ENDORSEMENTS

In this book Scott tells his story of how God restored his heart for Israel. Scott's story resonates with me on a personal level because the Lord has recently done a similar work in my heart. Like Scott, I have come to experience my faith, the Christian faith, in a more profound and personal way than I ever thought possible simply by understanding it the way it was meant to be understood. That is, within the framework of the original Hebraic faith—the spiritual, sociological, and historic context of the Hebrew people. My prayer is that through this book you'll have a fresh encounter with the Messiah, and that your faith would explode with new meaning as you see it anew. My hope is that God will burden your heart for His people and restore in the church a renewed vision to fulfill its calling to "provoke Israel to jealousy" (Romans 11:11).

—Stovall Weems, Pastor
Celebration Church
Jacksonville, Florida

Scott Volk is my friend. He's uncomplicated, unusually friendly, even to a total stranger. He is passionately in love with his family, his friends, and his God. He is generous, lighthearted, and given to communication as an art form. Why these words about him and his personality? Because I don't want you to make the mistake of reading the first few paragraphs of this book and dismiss it as being too simple, not meaty enough, or shallow. And because like this author, underneath the easygoing demeanor lies some very deep waters that have weathered storms that have cast too many others on the rocks...never to sail again.

Please read every page, consider the questions and answers offered here, and I bet you will find yourself saying something like, "That makes good sense now that you mention it!" You may even find yourself coming back again and again to use this work as a reference and guide. Yes, it's true, Yeshua is the Jewish Messiah who came for the lost sheep of the House of Israel, and He also loves you with the exact same passion and fire. The question is, do you love Him enough to love today's lost sheep of the House of Israel?

—Paul Wilbur
Messianic Recording Artist

Scott Volk has discovered a treasure to understanding the Scriptures. *Jesus Was Not a Christian* will open the reader's heart and mind to understand the Scriptures from a Hebraic perspective, igniting a fresh passion to embrace the Jewish Jesus. This book is for every believer who desires a fresh encounter with the Messiah of the Bible.

—Ward Simpson, President
God TV

I would recommend *Jesus Was Not a Christian* even if I didn't know Scott. However, I do know him and can happily say that this book reflects Scott's personality and character. A result of his profound wrestling with God, this book is engaging, winsome, honest, knowledgeable, and insightful. It is a perfect introduction to help disciples discover the biblical origins of their faith. The reality is that most of the Church has forgotten that Jesus is Jewish. This book is a good reminder of that basic truth and, through a beautiful birds-eye view of the Scriptures, explores the ramifications of the Father's heart for His people.

As I've watched Scott grow in his ministry, Together for Israel, I've been amazed at the favor that has flowed through him manifest in liberality. With the same openness of spirit, Scott's calling to reveal God's heart for Israel is evidenced in his writing. Scott does not only impart truth through his writing, he gives away his heart (1 Thessalonians 2:8).

In contrast with the faddish dismissal of Israel's importance in our nation's churches, this personable book is scrupulously biblical. Many realize that conservative Christian support for the Jewish people is under systematic attack. It can no longer be taken for granted. In the light of this, *Jesus Was Not a Christian* will help fortify, educate, and inoculate the Church against this ancient invidious hatred.

I intend to purchase numerous copies to give away. I expect it to inform, aid in intercession, and inspire responsible action.

—Pastor David Harwood, Author
For the Sake of the Fathers and *God's True Love*

Scott Volk is a gem of a brother in Christ. I am honored to call him "friend." I have a deep appreciation for his heart and his sense of mission. His new book is an invitation to realize that indeed the Savior of the World, Jesus our Messiah, was a descendent of Abraham, Isaac, and Jacob. He was a Hebrew; He was a Jew. In His conversation with the woman of Samaria, Jesus makes it clear that "salvation is of the Jews." Jesus IS our salvation. The Jewish roots of the Gospel are uncontested as far as the grand narrative of Scripture is concerned. The term "Christian" doesn't even appear in the primitive Church until the Church in Antioch was emerging in Gentile territory, where the disciples were first called "Christians." Scott invites you on a journey through the Sacred Text with an objective of inviting you to see the Story of the ancient faith with fresh eyes and fresh appreciation for the Jewish roots of the Gospel. Scott will invite you to develop great hope for a glorious future both for the Jews as well as the Gentiles. After all, Paul tells us that the Gospel is to be preached to the Jew first, and then to the Gentiles. Scott's words, if you take them to heart, will inspire your faith and hope for the rich possibilities revealed in the promises of God as it relates to a glorious future, which Paul foresaw for the nations and for Israel, with great assurance by the Spirit.

—Bishop Mark Chironna, PhD
Church on the Living Edge

Scott Volk is a dear friend. He is a tremendous voice and incredible man of God. He has taken the time to obey the Lord in putting together a much-needed resource for all who truly love Jesus. By discovering the biblical origins of our faith, the content found here will greatly challenge you to love Jesus, as He is, and not just the created idea of who He is. The topics discussed throughout will provide the necessary biblical insight to frame in the conversation in a way that is confronting and inviting, simultaneously. This book will stir your heart, open your eyes, and cause you to fall more deeply in love with Jesus and His mission, pertaining to Israel and the nations of the earth.

—Michael Dow, President
Burning Ones

Jesus Was Not a Christian is a clear, concise, and engaging read that will open your eyes to a biblical truth lost to the Church for centuries. Anyone who cares about the return of Jesus should read this book.

—Jonathan Bernis, Host
Jewish Voice with Jonathan Bernis

Scott Volk is a man who has given his life to partner with the Church for the salvation of Israel. His clear message and a prophetic voice come through powerfully in *Jesus Was Not a Christian*. In a time when anti-Semitism is rising around the world, more than ever, the Church needs to understand God's heart for the Jewish people and the nation of Israel. I highly recommend this timely book to every Christian.

—Evangelist Daniel Kolenda, President
Christ for all Nations

Everyone who knows Scott Volk loves him, with very good reason. Scott is a servant with a big pastoral heart. Beyond his commendable character, however, he is also a man of tremendous theological clarity with a lifetime of wisdom to offer. As Christians globally continue to awaken to the Jewish roots of our faith, it is imperative that we listen to the right teachers who have been raised up and anointed by the Lord to speak into this very critical subject. *No doubt, Scott is a father who we would all do well to listen to.* For anyone who desires to better understand the very Jewish context of the Bible, the life of Jesus, and their role in this unfolding story, this book will become a welcome and essential addition to their library.

—Joel Richardson
New York Times Best-Selling Author

I just finished reading *Jesus Was Not a Christian* by Scott Volk and Robert Gladstone and enjoyed their fresh approach to the study of Jesus' Jewishness and God's plan for Israel. I loved the combination of biblical and historical studies and the warmth of their stories, especially Scott's personal testimony woven throughout the book. I was completely drawn in by the coherent sweep of the story of Israel's redemption as Scott and Bob take us through on a journey through biblical and Jewish history from the Old

Testament to the New and then beyond to the formation of the modern state of Israel. This book would be a wonderful tool for family devotions, an adult Sunday school class, or for believers who are wanting a better understanding of their spiritual heritage and connection to the Jewish people. Scott's love for Israel and his people is evident from the book which led him to begin Together for Israel, a ministry that helps others develop this same love and enables Jewish and Gentile believers to put that love into action through serving needy Israelis. Thank you so much, Scott and Robert, for taking the time to share this book and the message of Jesus the Jewish Messiah with whomever has the joy of reading the book.

—Dr. Mitch Glaser, President
Chosen People Ministries

If you do not understand the Jewishness of Jesus, you will not understand the Jew and Israel.

If you are wrong in your understanding of the Jew and Israel, you will have your end-time understanding wrong and enter into further heresy!

—Sid Roth, Host
It's Supernatural!

FOREWORD BY MICHAEL L. BROWN, PhD

JESUS WAS
NOT
A CHRISTIAN

DISCOVERING THE BIBLICAL ORIGINS OF OUR FAITH

SCOTT VOLK
WITH ROBERT J. GLADSTONE, PhD

DEDICATION

This book is dedicated to some very special people in my life:

To my amazing wife: Beth Volk—your love for me and for our children is one of the most beautiful things I have ever witnessed.

To my amazing children: Alysa and Joey Signa (and baby Salem), Jonathan, Joseph and Jessa, Emily, and Olivia—being a father to all of you is simply one of the greatest joys of my life.

To my amazing parents: Shelly and June Volk— thank you for raising me to love the God of Abraham, Isaac, and Jacob.

To Together for Israel's amazing partners around the world: thank you for standing with our ministry and for being a demonstration of God's love to the lost sheep of the house of Israel.

To our amazing Jewish Messiah: Yeshua—thank You for opening my eyes and for giving me the privilege of proclaiming Your Name to the Nations.

TABLE OF CONTENTS

ACKNOWLEDGMENTS

I never realized how much went into writing a book until I sat down and simply started this adventure. From the time that the thought was first conceived in my mind, until the day the book was actually birthed, was approximately two years (which is the gestation period of an elephant!).

This book could not have been written if it were not for my dear friend, Robert Gladstone. His pen, coupled with his depth of scriptural understanding, added a dimension to this book that otherwise would have left it incomplete. Thank you for taking my skeletal chapters and adding both flesh and spirit to it.

No chapter was fully complete without the final okay of my wife, Beth. Thank you for proofreading, thank you for making sure that my thoughts were clearly articulated on the finalized chapters, and thank you for fully supporting me in this venture.

Michael Dow and his team at Burning Ones were able to turn a process that initially seemed overwhelming, into one that was joyful, easy, and without burden. Thank you for your partnership with us, your love for us, and for the way you made this whole process beautiful.

I was privileged to meet Dr. Michael Brown in the mid 1990s and have been blessed to work together ever since. I was honored to serve as his personal assistant and travel the world with him as he shared on themes related to Israel, the Church, and revival. Thank you, Mike, for pouring into me these last twenty-five years—I don't believe that I could have ever written a book with this theme without having you in my life.

And finally, I want to thank my parents, Shelly and June Volk, whose greatest desire was to see their children living for the Lord. If there is anything that is currently blossoming in my life, it is because of the seeds you have both planted as well as watered in my heart these last fifty-four years!

PREFACE

A few years ago, God began to stir my heart afresh for Israel. As I prayed about the purpose of that stirring, my good friend, Scott Volk, asked me to help him write this book. I thought his invitation was an answer to my prayer. So I agreed. And I'm very glad I did. My part in this book has been a profound honor with great reward. It gave me an opportunity to invest in Israel. It also pushed me further into God's heart for Israel. Now I see the "apple" of His eye just a little clearer. What a precious gift. I am humbled and grateful.

Scott and I met more than two decades ago in Pensacola, FL. For short periods of that time we were neighbors. For the bulk of that time we were coworkers in ministry. But for all of that time we have been close friends. Our families spent time together. Our children attended each other's birthdays and weddings. And our wives, Beth and Jeana, traded various insights into motherhood and homeschooling. Providence saw to it all. So for me, this collaboration is more than a little side project. It feels more like part of God's purpose for our friendship.

It's important that the Church understand God's heart for Israel. Much of Scott's ministry now is geared toward that very effort. Hence this book. Both of us wanted to expose readers to Jesus' Jewishness and Israel's role in the grand scheme of things. These two realities carry vast implications for the Church. But these two realities have also been ignored—even rejected—through much of the Church's history. Consequences of the ignorance have been regrettable. Consequences of the rejection have been absolutely tragic. As history moves toward its conclusion, the Church can no longer afford either one.

So the bottom line is this: we must see Israel from God's perspective. Jesus was the *Messiah* of *Israel* from the tribe of *Judah*. The roots of our faith are *Jewish*. They are not American, European, or anything else. And this is no mere fact of history. It relates to the very character of our present lives and the glory of our future. Knowing God's heart for Israel is crucial to biblical faith.

We need more than accurate doctrine on this matter. We must also feel God's burden. Paul did not just pray for Israel's salvation. He *desired* their salvation in his heart (Rom 10:1). That is why I think you'll find Scott's personal testimony fascinating and helpful. He is a Jew. Yet he needed God to open his heart to Israel in a new way. Now he sees his "kinsmen according to the flesh" more from God's perspective than his own. So must we.

The Bible clearly declares God's heart for Israel. So two chapters will focus on specific passages of Scripture. We thought it would be helpful simply to lay these passages out and discuss their implications. The Israel issue is not a matter of opinion. It flows directly from God's Word. He made an eternal covenant with Abraham, Isaac, and Jacob, and He spoke of that covenant often. But this covenant with Israel has a purpose larger than Israel. God's choice of that one nation was always meant to be a blessing to all nations. The Church, then, should pay attention to what God's Word says about His people, and therefore what it says about the nations.

Finally, a word about my favorite section of the book. As the process moved forward, Scott became stirred with the theme, "life from the dead." Three chapters near the end bear this theme. God, by nature, is the God who raises the dead. We see this pattern in everything He does, from Genesis to Revelation. As a result, no matter how far gone Israel may be, their full restoration is guaranteed. The God who calls light from the darkness will call Israel's life out of death. It's a compelling, life-altering truth. Which is why my part in those chapters changed my life. As I searched the Scriptures, read up on my history, and put a few words to paper, I found myself, figuratively, in the middle of Ezekiel's valley of dry bones. I could see their hopeless scattering. I smelled the decay. I cowered at the incurability. But then I heard the voice of the Lord and His prophet.

The bones came together. Bodies reassembled. Corpses came to life. And a mighty army stood for battle. From Judah's ancient return from exile, to the reestablished state of 1948, and into the glorious future, I caught a tiny glimpse of resurrection. It was sweet to the soul and healing to the bones. It gave me a new and deeper faith for Israel's salvation, the return of Jesus Christ, and the restoration of all things. "The night is nearly over; the day is almost here."

I pray you catch a glimpse of that too. *To life!*

—Bob Gladstone
Pesach, 5779

FOREWORD

Before I tell you about the book you're about to read, let me tell you about the man who wrote it. I have known Scott Volk since 1993 and have worked side by side with him since 1996. I can truly say he is one of the most giving, caring, and friendly people I know on the planet. That's why we dubbed him, "Everybody's best friend." He is a genuinely nice guy.

For years now, behind the scenes and in public, I have watched him put others first, epitomizing the philosophy of "live to give," demonstrating a real servant's heart. For Scott, this was as natural as breathing—nothing coerced or demanded. And that is why he wrote this book: not to receive something *from* you but to give something *to* you.

As you'll read in the pages that follow, although Scott is Jewish by birth, he did not have a "Jewish heart," by which I mean a special burden for the Jewish people or a special love for Israel. In fact, when sharing his testimony in years past, he would say something like, "My parents were Jewish," or, "I have a Jewish background." He wouldn't say the words, "I'm Jewish."

After all, he reasoned, why should he? He was a follower of Jesus, which meant he was a Christian, which meant that Jewish heritage and calling didn't matter. At least that's what he felt until God opened his eyes and changed his heart, calling him to leave his full-time pastoral job at our local congregation and to birth the Together for Israel ministry—a ministry which exists to give.

With amazement and thanksgiving, I have watched as the Lord put a unique burden on Scott, calling him to serve the hurting and the poor in Israel, including Jews and Arabs. (You should know that Scott's wife Beth is a full-blooded, Lebanese Arab.) And I have watched as the Lord has supernaturally backed this ministry, with favor and funding like nothing I have seen before— and whatever Scott gets, he gives away again.

Now, out of his love for God, for Israel, and for the Church, he has written this concise, clear, and compelling book. In it, he opens up the Scriptures that God opened up to him, beginning with the recognition that Yeshua, the Messiah of Israel and the Savior of the world, was not a Christian. (Does this surprise you? Then this book is absolutely for you.) Scott also explains God's eternal covenant with Israel, despite Israel's failings and sins, culminating in the grand finale in history: a massive harvest of souls from the nations and the salvation of Israel. Yes, Israel shall be saved!

But this book is not meant to be doctrinally divisive, nor is it meant to be an in-depth theological treatise. The purpose of the book is to convey God's heart to you—His heart for the Jewish people—until God's heart becomes your heart. And when you realize that Israel exists because of the faithfulness of the Lord (rather than because of its own faithfulness), you will be encouraged. The God who has preserved the Jewish people through the millennia is the same God who promised to fulfill His purposes for the Church. He is faithful!

Scott will also give you practical steps to take to enable you to be one who blesses Israel—something that remains important in the sight of the Lord. Could it be that your standing with Israel today—not primarily in a political way but in a spiritual way— could be a key ingredient to Israel's ultimate salvation? Could we be nearing the time to favor Zion? Could you be a part of it?

If that's your desire, turn the page (or, if you're reading the e-book, click away), and may the God and Father of Israel change your heart and enlighten your mind as you read.

—Dr. Michael L. Brown, author,
*Our Hands Are Stained with Blood: The Tragic Story of
the 'Church' and the Jewish People*;
host of the *Line of Fire* radio broadcast

INTRODUCTION

As Scott's wife, I have observed the journey of a man who avoided any form of Jewish ministry to one who has birthed not only a Jewish ministry, but one that seeks to help *others* see the importance of God's heart for Israel and His people. As a Lebanese believer in Jesus, this understanding of Israel's significance was never a part of my upbringing.

I grew up in a loving, Catholic home, learning about Jesus and my need for Him; and He became the center of my life. As an adult, I attended various denominational and nondenominational churches and grew immensely in my Christian walk. In each of these places, I did not hear a sermon on the importance of Jesus being Jewish or of Israel still being a significant nation in God's eyes.

Scott's parents, both Messianic Jews, had an in-depth understanding of these topics; but when discussions such as these arose, I seemed to feel they didn't apply to me and didn't enter into them. My lack of understanding played a significant role in my lack of interest. Ironically, Scott, also a Messianic Jew, didn't have an interest in the subject either. As the lead pastor of our church, Scott had never spoken a message on the importance of Israel.

You will read in the following pages of this book how the Lord apprehended Scott and completely grabbed his attention concerning Israel. At first, I had no desire to learn what Scott was learning. Then Scott taught a class on Jewish Roots at our church's ministry school, and I attended it. As Scott clearly laid out the significance of what the Bible has to say about Israel, my mind and heart started to see with clarity. Now, I want everyone to understand the Lord's heart for Israel and especially Israel's role in the Messiah's return.

I had the honor to read the chapters of this book as they were being written. For someone who was clueless about the subject a few years ago, I read these chapters hoping that someone who was as clueless as I was would comprehend the subject of this book. I truly believe that this book does just that. It clearly lays out why God needed to choose one nation, Israel, to fulfill His plan of salvation, why Jesus needed to be Jewish, and why the Church needs to play a role in Israel's salvation.

—Beth Volk

CHAPTER 1

JESUS WAS NOT
A CHRISTIAN

You may look at the title of this chapter and think, "That's heresy!" Well, not only is it not heresy, but it illustrates a truth essential to our faith. The Church has been so duped into picturing Jesus as a blonde-haired, blue-eyed, fair-skinned, halo-bearing "Christian" figure, that there is little to no understanding that He is actually a Jew through and through!

If we really want to know Jesus—if we are more interested in Jesus Himself than people's opinions about Him—then we must see Him against the background of His own history and culture. Facts must rule fiction. Many modern believers operate under the subtle illusion that Jesus arose from the Christian history of the Western world.

They might not actually say it that way. Most Christians know that, technically, Jesus was a Jew.

But they don't know how to process that information into something—or someone—they can relate to. So they view Jesus through the lens of their Christian tradition. To them, Jesus' Jewishness is an oddity—an aberration of history with no real relevance to their faith.

Yet truth insists otherwise. Think about it like this. If someone thought you had parents different than your real parents, with totally different ethnic backgrounds and from completely different parts of the world—wouldn't you want to correct them? Don't people need to know the truth about your heritage if they want to know *you?* There may be nothing wrong with those other people or their ethnic backgrounds. But they are not *your* parents, and that is not *your* background. It's just not *you.*

How much more important is it to know the true heritage of our Savior! Jesus did not start a Christian religion in fourth century Rome. He was not born in Europe during the Reformation, nor did He arrive in America with the Pilgrims. He never went to church, nor did He found any of our Christian denominations. *Jesus was not a Christian.*

But this certainly does not mean "Christian" is a bad word. "Christian" means "one who belongs to the Christ." I wholeheartedly embrace the term when it refers to a true follower of Jesus (rather than someone who merely affiliates with the Christian religion). Jesus' disciples adopted the title with honor since they were first called "Christians" in ancient Antioch (Acts 11:26; see also Acts 26:28; 1 Pet 4:16).

I thank God for the great impact authentic Christians have made on world history. But many modern Christians have viewed Jesus through the filter of their own, later Christian traditions, rather than through Jesus' own Jewish heritage. Though they may not mean to do it, they effectively see Jesus as a Christian from their own denomination, rather than as a first century Jew.

Recently I spoke to our congregation in North Carolina on the topic of "God's Heart For Israel." As I prepared for the message, the thought that "Jesus was not a Christian" struck me for the first time. I wanted to express this in my message, but was hesitant to make a public statement I had never heard anyone else make. So I called Dr. Michael Brown, a dear friend and biblical scholar, and asked him if this was an accurate statement. His response was, "Are you kidding me? Of course Jesus was not a Christian. There were no such things as Christians back then!"

What a wake-up call. Here I was, uneasy about making a public statement that "Jesus was not a Christian" because it felt unorthodox and contro- versial—even harsh. But in reality it was a perfectly accurate biblical, logical, and historical fact! Why did I hesitate?

I hesitated because I was still chipping away at the stained glass window through which I had viewed Jesus as a product of Christianity, rather than as the Jewish Messiah. Years earlier, I had a personal awakening to my own Jewishness. But I still did not realize just how much I had "gentilized" the King of the Jews. Perhaps we need a radical paradigm shift in the Church to see Jesus as He really is, and to appreciate that His original mission was "for the lost sheep of the house of Israel" (Matt 15:24).

PERHAPS WE NEED A RADICAL PARADIGM SHIFT IN THE CHURCH TO SEE JESUS AS HE REALLY IS.

This is why Jesus' Jewishness is so essential. We must recover the foundation and root of our faith in order to have an accurate understanding of God's purpose for Israel and the world. An insufficient grasp of this crucial fact will not only marginalize Jesus' mission while on earth, but will also marginalize our call as the Church to provoke Israel to jealousy. Jesus did not come to earth and shed His blood to start a new religion called Christianity; He came to fulfill the Scriptures as the Messiah of Israel and the Savior of the world.

Let's look at some simple facts from the Gospels, and see how Jewish Jesus really was:

JESUS HAD JEWISH ANCESTRY

The genealogy of Jesus in Matthew 1:1 states,

"The record of the genealogy of Jesus the Messiah, the son of David, the son of Abraham."

Matthew then traces Jesus' family tree from the great patriarch of the Hebrews, Abraham, through King David, to the birth of Jesus as the Jewish Messiah (1:2-16). Although this may seem elementary, there was not one "Christian" in Jesus' entire lineage! As Dr. Brown said, they didn't exist yet.

> HE CAME TO FULFILL THE SCRIPTURES AS THE MESSIAH OF ISRAEL AND THE SAVIOR OF THE WORLD.

In fact, the reason Matthew began his gospel with Jesus' Jewish genealogy was to make this point from the outset: Jesus was thoroughly Jewish. The title "Son of Abraham" meant He belonged to Abraham's family and faith. And "Son of David" meant He belonged to David's royal lineage, qualifying Him to be the Jewish Messiah.

Jesus was born a Jew with the Hebrew name, Yeshua. His earthly, adoptive father descended from the tribe of Judah and the house of David (Matt 1:2-16). We know him as Joseph, but in Hebrew his name was pronounced "Yosef." Jesus' mother was also a Jew descended from Judah and David (Luke 2:4-5; Rom 1:3). Though it's common to refer to her as "the Virgin Mary," her name was actually Miriam—the same name as Moses' sister (Num 26:59).

JESUS HAD A JEWISH UPBRINGING

Yosef and Miriam raised their firstborn son, Yeshua, exactly the way good Jewish parents would. Judaism, after all, was no token religion for them; it was their way of life. God's Law—the Torah—governed every aspect of their lives. They were proud members of God's covenant people, fully immersed in the culture of Judaism and awaiting the hope of Israel.

Thus the Founder of "Christianity" was not raised in a Christian home. He was raised in a Jewish home. Young Yeshua grew up in a Jewish village celebrating the seven feasts of Israel, as well as Hanukkah and Purim. Year after year, He joined His parents and other Jewish pilgrims making the journey to Jerusalem for Passover. Jesus would sing the songs of "ascents" with the crowd as they climbed the paths to Mount Zion.

JESUS WAS NOT A CHRISTIAN

Perhaps Jesus accompanied Joseph when He brought the lamb to the priests for sacrifice. Or when He was older, assuming Joseph died before Jesus left home, it is possible that the duty of bringing the family's sacrifice to the temple fell to Him.

THE FOUNDER OF "CHRISTIANITY" WAS NOT RAISED IN A CHRISTIAN HOME.

Then He would eat the feast with family and fellow pilgrims. He would remember His people's deliverance from Egypt. He would remember Israel's hope. And He would know that, one day, the entire celebration would be fulfilled in His own death.

Jesus' upbringing was very Jewish. But we would expect nothing else for a Jewish young man, with Jewish parents, living in first century Israel, who also happened to be the Jewish Messiah.

JESUS HAD A JEWISH MISSION

Did you know that the God of Israel originally promised the New Covenant to "the house of Israel and the house of Judah" (Jer 31:31-33)? Some people think that the New Testament is for Christians, while the Old Testament is for Jews. But actually, *both* testaments are Jewish books. The New Testament is a collection of writings that proclaims the New Covenant originally promised to Jews in the Old Testament!

That is why, during His ministry on earth, Jesus said, "I was sent only to the lost sheep of the house of Israel" (Matt 15:24). When He sent His disciples on their first mission, He told them, "Do not go in the way of the Gentiles, and do not enter any city of the Samaritans; but rather go to the lost sheep of the house of Israel" (Matt 10:6).

JESUS' MISSION WAS A JEWISH MISSION.

That may sound a little cruel on the surface. But Jesus was not rejecting other nations. He was remaining faithful to *His* nation, Israel. God had promised Israel a New Covenant, under which He would forgive their sins, rescue them from their enemies, fill them with His Spirit, and be their King.

So Jesus came to earth to fulfill these promises to His people. Then, after He died and rose again, He planned to send His Jewish apostles into the world to welcome all nations into His Kingdom with open arms—if they would believe. But in order to advance a mission into all nations, Jesus *first* had to carry out a mission to *His* nation. Jesus' mission was a Jewish mission.

In fact, did you know that the twelve apostles were all Jews? Jesus chose Jewish men to fulfill His Jewish mission, and take His Jewish message to the nations. I love how *The Jewish New Testament* describes Jesus' choosing twelve disciples to be His special messengers:

> It was around that time that Yeshua went out to the hill country to pray, and all night he continued in prayer to God. When day came, he called his *talmidim* and chose from among them twelve to be known as emissaries: Shim'on, whom he named Kefa; Andrew, his brother; Ya'akov; Yochanan; Philip; Bar-Talmai; Mattityahu; T'oma; Ya'akov Ben Halfai; Shim'on, the one called the Zealot; Y'hudah Ben-Ya'akov; and Y'hudah from K'riot, who turned traitor (Luke 6:12-16).[1]

That has such a unique ring to it! Normally we would read this passage through more "Christian" ears. But in the JNT translation, "Peter" is "Kefa," "John" is "Yochanan," "Matthew" is "Mattityahu," and "James" is "Ya'akov." As odd as these names may sound, they were the actual, Jewish names of the twelve apostles. Each one was a Jew because Yeshua, the Jewish Messiah, was on a mission to fulfill God's promises to His Jewish people.

JESUS WAS A JEWISH KING

Actually, Jesus was *the* Jewish King. He was, and is, the Messiah of Israel, the King of the Jews. Did you know that people actually confess this all the time, even when they don't realize it? Whenever people refer to "Jesus Christ," they declare that He is the King of Israel. Whether they say His name as a curse, as a simple reference, or as a testimony to their Lord and Savior, "Jesus Christ" means, "Jesus is the Messiah"—and that means, King of Israel.

"JESUS CHRIST" MEANS, "JESUS IS THE MESSIAH"— AND THAT MEANS, KING OF ISRAEL.

The English word, "Christ," comes from the Greek word, *Christos*. And *Christos* translates the Hebrew word, *Mashiach*, or "Messiah." So "Jesus Christ" really means, "Jesus the Messiah." The word "Messiah" means, "anointed one." It comes from the ancient Israelite practice of applying oil to the man God chose to be the king of His people.

For example, when the Lord showed Samuel the prophet that He had chosen David to be king of Israel, Samuel poured oil over David's head. Then God sent His Spirit to rest on David in a special way. So David was "anointed" with oil by Samuel, and "anointed" with the Spirit by God, to rule as king over Israel.

Early in his life, David was a lowly shepherd boy in Bethlehem. But he was also a "man after God's own heart"—the kind of man God wanted as His king. David became a skilled musician, a wise sage, a mighty warrior, and a great ruler. Though he made some terrible mistakes during his reign, he still returned to the Lord and came to embody Israel's glory. In fact, God declared that His kings would only come from David's family.

So during the days of their oppression, Israel increasingly longed for the "Messiah," "the Son of David," to appear. That special King from David's family would rescue them from their enemies, bring them freedom, and rule them in righteousness. That is what the word "Christ" meant to Jews living in Jesus' time. And that is what the word means today. It is not a Gentile word; it is a Jewish word. It is not Jesus' "Christian" last name; it is the title of His Jewish royalty.

Thus Matthew called his gospel, "the record of the genealogy of Jesus the Messiah, the son of David" (Matt 1:1). When the angels announced Jesus' birth, they said, "Today in the city of David there has been born for you a Savior, who is the Messiah, the Lord" (Luke 2:11). And later the Magi, following a star to Jerusalem, asked, "Where is He who has been born King of the Jews?" (Matt 2:2). No wonder Herod tried to kill the Child. Rome had declared *Herod* "king of the Jews." And there could be only one king!

Years later, during His ministry, Jesus asked His disciples to acknowledge His identity. Simon Peter responded, "You are the Messiah" (Matt 16:16). When the Jewish leaders had Jesus arrested and brought to the Roman governor, Pontius Pilate, they accused Him of pretending to be "the Messiah"—a Jewish king who threatened the Roman Empire (Luke 23:2). When Pilate had Jesus crucified, he nailed a sign to the top of the cross that said, "This is Yeshua, the King of the Jews" (Matt 27:37).

JESUS WAS BORN A JEW, RAISED A JEW, LIVED LIKE A JEW, AND RULES AS KING OF THE JEWS.

Then after Jesus was raised from the dead, He explained to His disciples that the "Messiah had to suffer and enter His glory" (Luke 24:26). After His ascension, His apostles proclaimed to Israel, and then the nations, "Jesus is the Messiah, the Lord of all" (Acts 10:36). Even in the heavens, before the throne of God, Jesus is known as the "Lion of the Tribe of Judah, the Root of David" (Rev 5:5). And when He returns to earth, He will bear the name, "King of kings and Lord of lords" (Rev 19:16).

So Jesus was born as Messiah, King of the Jews. His enemies and disciples acknowledged His claim to be the King of the Jews. He died as the King of the Jews. He rose again as the King of the Jews. And He is coming again as the King of the Jews—and the Lord of all nations.

Jesus was indeed not a Christian. Nor was He the Gentile leader of Christian religion. Jesus was born a Jew, raised a Jew, lived like a Jew, and rules as King of the Jews. And as King of the Jews, Jesus is also the Sovereign over *all* nations. Or, to say that in terms of the earliest Church's confession, "Yeshua the Messiah is Lord!"

CHAPTER 2

GOD'S HEART FOR ISRAEL

The story of God and Israel is a love story. It is often marked by sin and tragedy, broken covenant and judgment—but it is still a love story. As told by Ezekiel, the narrative begins when a great King finds a poor, orphaned girl. He rescues her, cares for her, and clothes her in royal garments. Adorned with glory, her true beauty shines and the King falls in love with her. He marries her and makes her His queen.

But when the orphan-turned-monarch gains worldwide fame, she prostitutes herself to the nations. The defiled queen suffers immeasurably for her adulteries. But the King declares that His covenant with her is eternal, and His love will one day eclipse His anger. On that day, their marriage will be restored (Ezek 16).

The prophets, like those quoted above, knew this love story well. As close friends of Yahweh (God's name in the Old Testament), they shared His Spirit and therefore understood His emotions. Even as they heard God's words of judgment, they also felt His broken heart for His wayward people. Israel's prophets grasped God's faithful love to restore His nation again. That is why their prophecies always came back to Israel's promised, glorious future. The prophets did more than share God's messages with Israel. They also shared God's heart for Israel.

PROPHETIC PEOPLE

And now more than ever, so must we! The Church must be a prophetic people who not only repeat God's words, but also share His heart. As followers of Jesus we have the same Spirit as the prophets. We have intimate, internal access to God's heart for Israel—if we would only avail ourselves of that friendship. True love for God means we pursue His heart above our own. And when we do, we will discover a treasure trove of affections toward Israel. Yet the Church remains divided over God's relationship with Israel.

Some hold that the Church has replaced Israel, so there is no longer need to care specifically about their place in history and salvation. Others recognize God's special calling on Israel, but they view Israel as a concept rather than real people who need the Church's prayers and tangible witness. Loving the Jews for them is more of a spiritual fashion statement than a practical burden. Still others ignore the issue of Israel completely. Even if they believe in Israel's special calling, they do not care.

But none of these reflects God's heart for Israel. That is why we must read the Scriptures afresh, by the Spirit and without prejudice, asking the Lord to open our hearts to His burden. We need the Spirit to do a fresh work in our hearts if we want to apprehend God's heart for Israel. Which is exactly what happened to me.

> WE NEED THE SPIRIT TO DO A FRESH WORK IN OUR HEARTS IF WE WANT TO APPREHEND GOD'S HEART FOR ISRAEL.

MY STORY

I did not understand God's heart for Israel until I was about forty years old. Like the third group mentioned above, I firmly believed in Israel's unique calling and purpose. But I did not carry a burden for the Jewish people. Strange, I know, coming from a Jewish man who grew up in a Jewish family, whose Jewish parents received Yeshua as the Jewish Messiah when he was still very young. Yet there I was: an outsider looking in. The theology in my head agreed with Israel's special place, while the affections in my heart did not. But why was I so dispassionate toward my own people?

Ever since I was a kid, Jewish ministry turned me off. Those with a "burden for Israel," to my young mind, were strange. Most of the Messianic congregations I attended in my youth seemed filled with non-Jewish people. They appeared to be more interested in looking and sounding Jewish than carrying an actual burden for Israel. They waved flags, wore prayer shawls and kippas, celebrated the Jewish feasts, and quoted Hebrew phrases like magic formulas. They gave off a strange vibe to me. Whoever didn't call Jesus "Yeshua" and worship on the "Shabbat" lacked spiritual substance.

But I always felt they lacked substance. I could not understand why Gentiles would want to dress like Jews, talk like Jews, and even eat like Jews. Worse, many of these ministries related to Israel seemed more politically motivated than biblically motivated. All of this made me very uncomfortable. So I stayed clear of anything that resembled Israel-related ministry.

If that weren't enough, even my extended family confirmed my reticence toward "Jewish ministry." Though I dearly love my Jewish relatives, it was not always easy to be around them. My grandparents' Jewish retirement community in South Florida felt like an ongoing Seinfeld episode. The conversations could be downright hilarious. But they also reflected a way of thinking very different than my own. It was nothing personal, I just couldn't relate to it—at all.

Don't get me wrong. In spite of my discomfort toward Jewish family and ministry, I was still always proud of my Jewish heritage. The men who have had the biggest influence on me were all sold-out Jewish believers who carried a heart for Israel and longed to see their kinsmen saved. Which makes it all the more strange that I still could not relate to the burden they carried. When they would speak of God's heart for Israel or the Church's role in Israel's salvation, no chord was struck in my heart. I wished they would speak about something more "current" or "relevant."

My burden focused more on the local church. As someone with a shepherd's heart, I was most fulfilled pastoring a healthy congregation, cultivating relationships, and influencing people through my life and teaching. I only wanted to serve God's flock—whatever their ethnic background. Looking back, I'm amazed at my detachment from God's heart for Israel. I was a Messianic Jew with deep respect for other Messianic Jews who carried a burden for the Jewish people. Yet I had no burden myself. I had no heart for Israel.

But one day that began to change.

FINALLY ENTERING THE LAND

I had little desire to visit Israel until my first trip in 2002—when I was thirty-seven years old. I accompanied my friend Michael Brown who was speaking at a conference in Jerusalem. While in the city, I connected with an old friend who led tours in Israel. He encouraged me to bring over my own tour group so I could experience Israel more fully and bless others with the same experience. It sounded like a nice idea; I was mildly interested. But without a real burden for Israel, it took me three years to heed his advice.

When I finally put the tour together, I determined that it would be different than the "Jewish ministry" that made me so uncomfortable. I did not want to play into the popular Christian hype surrounding Israel that didn't connect with the real issues, and more importantly, the real people. Christians should not walk around Israel as if it were a giant pop-up book just for American pilgrims. Of course we would check out the great biblical sites. But we would also make a couple of stops that would expose us to the complex realities of modern Jews and Arabs in Israel. Little did I know that was exactly where God planned to confront me with some of those realities, and begin a new work in my heart.

JESUS AND THE CHILDREN
OF TIBERIAS

One of our stops took us to a home for poor children in Tiberias, a town on the western shore of the Sea of Galilee. As we distributed Hanukkah gifts to those beautiful young people (some of whom did not know when their next hot meal would be served), I heard the still, small voice of the Lord whisper a familiar passage of Scripture to me: "Inasmuch as you've done it to one of the least of these my brothers, you've done it to Me" (Matt 25:40).

The words interrupted my thoughts and began to open my eyes. I had read that passage many times. But for the first time I saw that it spoke specifically about the lost lambs of Israel's house—just like these children. In that moment I began to understand God's heart for Israel. I felt His love for the Jewish people like I never had before. I started to look at Israel through a whole new lens.

Previously I looked at "Israel" through a filter of strange people that made me uncomfortable. But I didn't really see "Israel" at all. Then when the Holy Spirit spoke a word to my heart, I began to grasp God's burden for Israel—a burden I tuned out for years. The entire course of my life started to shift.

Right then and there I made myself available to the Lord for Zion's sake. I did not know where that commitment would take me, but trusted that God would unfold the next steps in His time. Until then, Beth and I decided to start a ministry to raise money for Jewish and Arab believers in Israel. It would channel resources from Christians into solid ministries that reached the poor and evangelized the lost in Israel. We also continued to lead annual tours—all while pastoring a congregation in North Carolina.

PROPHETIC DESTINY

After five years of holding that pattern, the Lord spoke again. It was during my flight home from one of our Israel tours. This time He sealed the deal. The Shepherd who guides us down paths of righteousness altered my course and declared my destiny.

It seemed the Lord came and sat right next to me on the plane, pointed His finger at me, and said, "You're a Jew. I've called you to the lost sheep of the house of Israel." The words flowed into my inner man with crystal clarity. My heart changed. Right there on an airplane soaring through the sky, I entered into my purpose. My own Jewishness, and my ultimate calling, suddenly became real to me. I did not realize it, but the Lord had this moment planned my whole life. (And I had no idea Jesus flew Delta!)

Just as the prophets felt God's heart for Israel by the Spirit, so must we. In that moment on the plane, the Holy Spirit poured God's love for Israel into my heart. What was doctrinal and cerebral became a warm, breathing reality inside of me. Since then I have read the Scriptures about Israel in a whole new light. Now my entire ministry is devoted to helping others understand God's heart for Israel.

> JUST AS THE PROPHETS FELT GOD'S HEART FOR ISRAEL BY THE SPIRIT, SO MUST WE.

That is why I shared this story with you. The Church today needs a similar, prophetic connection with God's love for this nation. Only by the Spirit can we feel His heart for Israel. Maybe you are like me. You believe in Israel's biblical destiny but cannot muster a burden for it. Or perhaps you completely reject Israel's place in God's heart and history. Or you may simply not understand enough about it to carry the Lord's burden. Let me encourage you. Continue to read this book with an open, prayerful heart. As a follower of Jesus, you possess God's Spirit. That means you can share His heart for Israel. Ask Him for that. Read the Scriptures in the light of God's love for His people.

Perhaps He would even enable you to visit the Land to give you an experience like He gave me. Of all people, we Christians who possess the Holy Spirit should share God's heart for Israel.

GOD'S HEART FOR ISRAEL

The Jewish people are more than theological statistics or spiritual fashion statements for Christians. They are real people with a special call, even when they resist God's plan. But God still sees in them something so treasured and lovely that His heart remains fastened to them till they see the morning light of their salvation. They remain His chosen people.

GOD WILL FULFILL ALL OF HIS PROMISES SPECIFICALLY TO ISRAEL.

"For you are a people holy to the Lord your God. The Lord your God has chosen you out of all the peoples on the face of the earth to be his people, his treasured possession" (Deut 7:6).

We know about Israel's historic rebellion against the Lord. We know that the vast majority of them have rejected their Messiah. For such sins they have suffered greatly. God's special love for Israel does not by itself qualify them to be saved or fulfill their destiny. They must repent and believe in Jesus like anyone else.

But one day that will happen! "All Israel will be saved" (Rom 11:26). God will fulfill all of His promises specifically to Israel. They have not been replaced; they have not been rejected forever. Even after a long history of rebellion that broke God's heart and distorted His testimony, God is still committed to this special people. His loyalty does not ultimately depend on Israel's behavior. It depends on the covenant He made with them out of the burning love in His heart.

God has a heart for Israel.

PEOPLE OF THE SPIRIT

Jesus told us not to "judge according to appearance, but [to] judge with righteous judgment" (John 7:24). People with the Holy Spirit are expected to see things from God's point of view rather than their own. No issue tests the Church like Israel. No issue forces us out of our own prejudices and agenda more effectively than the "controversy of Zion" (Isa 34:8). The Lord has laid down a stone that is choice and precious, but also vexed. This is not going to change. In spite of Israel's failures, God's covenant love burns for them and He faithfully longs for their return.

Since God's Spirit abides within the Church, we should also long for Israel's return. But sadly this is not always the case. As I said earlier, the Church is torn over Israel. Just because we have the Spirit does not mean we automatically share God's perspective. We must still step beyond our opinions and cultivate God's perspective through the Spirit. Put another way: if we really want to know God's heart, we must pursue His heart.

For me it all started when I took a few small steps toward God's burden for Israel (and even that came after the gentle encouragement of a friend). Then the Lord began to unveil His heart for Israel to me. After only a few small steps! This is why I'm writing this book. I want to be that kind of friend to you. I want to nudge you closer to God's heart for Israel. Maybe this is why so many Christians divide over the "Israel issue." Perhaps our opinions about Israel exceed our prophetic connection to God's heart for Israel.

David was "a man after God's own heart" (1 Sam 13:14). That means he wanted to understand God's affections, and he cared about God's desires more than his own. Isn't that what any wholesome relationship is about? Love does not seek its own desires. Love seeks the heart of the beloved! I believe if we pursue God's heart this way, we will discover His passion for Israel the way David and the prophets did. And that passion will burn away our opinions, our apathy, and our unscriptural views about Israel.

CHAPTER 3

GOD'S HISTORIC LOVE FOR HIS PEOPLE: THE OLD TESTAMENT

Now you know my story. I'm so thankful that, like a close friend, the Lord opened up and shared His heart for Israel with me. The encounter changed my life. Not only did it point me toward my destiny, but it also made me a more complete follower of Jesus. After all, who was I to enjoy God's salvation while ignoring one of His greatest burdens? Why should I reap the benefits of Israel's Messiah while failing to pray for Israel's salvation? I was a shepherd to God's people, the Church. Yet I did not grasp the Great Shepherd's heart for His lost Jewish sheep. But now I do. I'm grateful the Lord led me to discover His heart for Israel!

But my discovery was not simply a spiritual experience. It was also a biblical experience. When the Holy Spirit opened God's heart to me, He also opened the

Scriptures to me. I needed Jesus to do for me what He did for His disciples after His resurrection: "He opened their minds to understand the Scriptures" (Luke 24:45). I am so thankful He did that for me, too!

IF WE LOOK AT ISRAEL THROUGH A BIBLICAL LENS, WE WILL END UP LOVING BOTH ARABS AND JEWS.

Now when I read the Bible, passages about God's love for Israel jump off the page into my spirit. Words that used to be theological or historical facts are now living words in my heart. With the veil removed from my eyes, I have a fuller grasp of Scripture and a deeper knowledge of God Himself (Psa 119:18).

Because Israel and the Jewish people can be such volatile topics, it is essential that the Word of God be our foundation. Political viewpoints and human sentimentalities too often dictate how we interpret Scripture. If we look at Israel through a political lens, we will end up hating either Arabs or Jews (or both!). If we look at Israel through a biblical lens, we will end up loving both Arabs and Jews.

That is why I will take the next two chapters and highlight some key biblical passages that declare God's heart for Israel. My goal is to show you that God's covenant with Israel is not a matter of opinion. It is a matter of God's eternal Word!

Before we dive into these Scriptures, I encourage you to take a moment and pray. Pray that, like the disciples mentioned above, Jesus would open your mind to understand the Scriptures. Say with the psalmist: "Open my eyes that I may see wonderful things in your law" (Psa 119:18). Pray that as you read God's Word about Israel, you will understand what He means and feel His burden. Pray that if you've had any misconceptions about Israel, the Lord would reveal them to you and help you understand His perspective. I believe God will answer your prayers. In fact, I believe He will bless you for praying these prayers simply because it means you are pursuing His heart.

GOD'S HEART FOR ISRAEL IN THE OLD TESTAMENT

For thus says the Lord of hosts, "After glory He has sent Me against the nations which plunder you, for he who touches you, touches the apple of His eye" (Zech 2:8).

Stop for a moment and imagine God's saying to you: "You are the apple of my eye!" What a tender, vivid picture of His heart for Israel (which applies to all believers as well). For Him to call Zion the "apple of His eye" is both bold and personal. The image seeps with compassion, reflecting the affections of a proud, devoted father.

In the Hebrew Bible, the eye's pupil—translated "apple" in English—implies a love that watches over its beloved with an adoring, intense gaze. If Israel would look up into God's eyes, they would see their own reflection like a "tiny man" in the middle of His eyeball (Deut 32:10; Psa 17:8). They would know that they are watched, surrounded, protected, and loved. They would see themselves as the apple of His eye.

Zechariah originally used this phrase to describe a small group of Jews hundreds of years before Messiah. After decades of exile, the mighty Persian Empire allowed them to return to their homeland, rebuild their temple, and in a very limited way, restore their national identity. But people from the surrounding nations opposed them and forced them to stop building. So God sent the prophet Zechariah to remind them: "You're still the apple of God's eye. He is watching out for you and will protect you; keep building!"

That image of the apple, however, has a dual meaning. It applies both to Zion and Zion's enemies, but in two different ways. Those opposing the work of the Jewish returnees had no idea what they were getting into when they threatened God's beloved. Israel's tender, devoted Father was equally a passionate, protective Father. He also happened to be the Commander of heaven's vast army. Although Israel's enemies must have felt powerful, they had no clue about the hornets' nest they were stirring.

ISRAEL, BE COMFORTED: GOD WILL WATCH OVER YOU AND ONE DAY SAVE YOU WHEN YOU TURN TO HIM.

Zechariah's words of comfort to the Jews also acted as a warning to their foes. When you touch those who live in the middle of God's eye, well, you poke God in the eye. Are you sure that's what you want? Are you prepared for the reply of a protective Father and all-powerful military leader who just watched you simultaneously strike His son and shove a stick in His eye?

Modern nations should still heed this warning. If God's "eye" does not change, neither does the object of His gaze. Israel, be comforted: God will watch over you and one day save you when you turn to Him. Enemies of Zion, be warned: God has a heart for the people He has chosen and ever watches over.

And who is like your people Israel—the one nation on earth whose God went out to redeem a people for Himself, and to make a name for yourself (1 Chron 17:21, NIV)?

Let's look at this verse in context to feel its weight. King David is the one speaking. He had just received a staggering, life-altering prophecy about his destiny, as well as Israel's destiny. (More on that below.) Inspired by that word, it occurred to David with tremendous force that there simply is no nation on earth like Israel. They are utterly unique. God sought this nation—and no other nation—to make His great name famous in the earth.

That point is clear enough. But if we look a little closer at David's distinct perspective, it will give us more insight into God's heart for Israel.

First, notice how David describes the way God acted on Israel's behalf. He says God "went out" to redeem them. Think of how different heaven's beauty would be compared to the arid wastelands of the Middle Eastern desert. Yet Yahweh said to Moses in the burning bush, "I have come down to deliver My people" (Exod 3:8). Yes, God descended from heaven in person to join Moses, confront Pharaoh, and lead His people out of Egypt (see Psa 114).

This point was very special to David. David was not only a man after God's heart, but he also was a man who sought God's face (Psa 27:4). That means he loved God's presence. He called it the "fullness of joy" filled with "pleasures forever" (Psa 16:11). That is why he spent so much time alone with God and desired to build Him a house.

So it was important to David that God did not send a messenger to rescue His people. He came down Himself. He was not repulsed by their slavish conditions. He visited them, live and in person, to conquer the Egyptians and escort His people to freedom. Then He remained with them in the desert as their Shepherd and fellow Nomad, leading them patiently through the wilderness for forty years. David knew that God's presence with Israel in those conditions meant they were very dear to Him. They became God's dwelling place and representative to the other nations.

But why Israel? Why would God go so far out of His way to liberate them? They had no global prominence, no homeland, no military, and no political influence. What was so attractive about them for God to choose them and personally redeem them? They were slaves. As far as the world could see, Israel was a nonentity—a trivial people serving the interests of an empire of real importance.

But here is why David's perspective helps us see God's heart for Israel. As Paul would say centuries later, David learned by experience that "God has chosen the foolish things of the world to shame the wise" (1 Cor 1:26). David himself was totally insignificant in the eyes of the world. He was scorned by his own family and relegated to the lowliest tasks of his household. But like Israel, God chose him and made him great. When we consider David's story, we can see why he had such insight into God's heart for Israel.

God had sent a prophet named Samuel to Bethlehem to anoint a new king for Israel. He came to the house of a man named Jesse who had eight sons. David was one of those sons. Yet Jesse only had seven sons appear before the prophet. They were tall and distinguished—obvious choices to become king. But not David. As the youngest and smallest in stature and rank, he remained outside tending the sheep. His father did not even bother to mention him. Even Samuel thought one of the first seven must be God's choice. Then the Lord said to him, "Man looks at the outward appearance, but the Lord looks at the heart" (1 Sam 16:7).

After hearing there was still one forgotten son, Samuel insisted Jesse bring him in. What a sight that must have been. David enters the house like a child, reminding us of Israel in Egypt and looking totally unfit for royalty: young, short, unassuming, unkempt, and stained by work in the fields. To human eyes, he looked like an outcast. To heaven's eyes, he looked like a king. God spoke to Samuel: "Arise, anoint him; for this is he" (1 Sam 16:12).

God chose the foolish to shame the wise, the weak to shame the strong. No wonder David was fit to become Israel's king. Both were forgotten by the world and unimpressive by its standards. Yet for those very reasons, God chose them to make His name famous and discredit human arrogance. Just as Israel became God's chosen nation, David became their king. Despite his many faults and mistakes, he was the greatest king in history. He would become a prototype of the Messiah Himself.

But that's not all. As amazing as David's rags to riches story was, the Lord made it infinitely greater. Not only did God raise David from the shepherd's field to the palace, He also promised David that his family would rule Israel forever! God gave David the eternal dynasty over Israel. No king would ever rule Yahweh's kingdom except one of David's sons.

What an amazing promise! What a powerful legacy! Can you imagine God's sending a prophet to give you such a message: that your family would always be royalty, a lineage of kings chosen by God, to rule His people forever? This meant that even the Messiah, the ultimate king of Israel, would come from David's family. God did more than make David king. God promised him an eternal dynasty. David's name would be great forever.

Upon hearing such news, David was overcome with gratitude. He went aside and worshipped the Lord with one of the great prayers in the Bible. In fact, this was exactly the moment David spoke the words quoted above. That's what makes these words about God's heart for Israel so significant. David's experience opened his eyes to see Israel in a whole new light.

It inspired him to ask three questions in his prayer: "Who am I?... Who is like the Lord?... and Who is like your people, Israel?" (See 1 Chron 17:16-27.) Once David saw just how far the Lord brought him— from the shadows into eternal royalty—he also saw the Lord's eternal choice of Israel with far greater clarity. He realized just how important Israel was to God's heart and purposes. This is the "Davidic" message we too must understand.

Both David and Israel symbolize God's unique way of challenging a world full of arrogance. "He raises the poor from the dust and lifts the needy from the ash heap; he seats them with princes and has them inherit a throne of honor" (1 Sam 2:8). That is the way of God's Kingdom. It brings shame on the world's defiant, boastful claims, and gives God all the glory (Luke 10:21-22; 1 Cor 1:27-31). After all, what can the nations say when an overlooked shepherd boy becomes the greatest king in history—and a forefather of the eternal King? What can they say when an obscure nation of slaves overcomes the world's greatest civilization to become the people of destiny?

They can say nothing. God has chosen the very ones rejected by the world. That is why He has woven His promises to Israel together with His promises to David. They are forever intertwined. Now as long as David has a son on the throne, Israel remains God's specially chosen nation! And you know what? David has a son on the throne right now. That fact is the centerpiece of our Gospel. God has raised one of David's sons from the dead and seated Him at His right hand forever (Matt 1:1; Rom 1:1-4; Eph 1:19-23). His name is Yeshua. He is the one forever qualified to rule God's people, and is sitting on the throne in heaven as you read this. With David's greatest Son enthroned as Israel's final king, God's original promises to Israel are confirmed. David and his "son," Yeshua, have forever made it official. God has a heart for Israel.

"Though the mountains be shaken and the hills be removed, yet My unfailing love for you will not be shaken nor My covenant of peace be removed," says the Lord, who has compassion on you (Isa 54:10).

Scripture speaks often about the earth as a symbol of stability and security. Mountains and hills, in particular, embody the earth's strength. They are fixed, sturdy, and impervious to the forces of nature. What is powerful enough to shake huge mountains or remove deeply rooted hills?

Yet even if there were such forces to make mountains convulse and hills crumble, they still could never budge God's heart away from Israel! His love for that nation will never waver. His covenant with Jacob's will simply never fade. What more can He say to make His point and convince our minds? God's heart is forever connected to His beloved Israel.

HIS COVENANT WITH JACOB'S CHILDREN WILL SIMPLY NEVER FADE.

Yes, Israel's rebellion has invited God's judgment. But God has promised that these judgments will not last forever. His love is too great for His beloved nation. Even today, much of that nation continues to reject its Messiah and remains backslidden by God's standards. But the Lord's love will outrun His anger! "In a surge of anger I hid my face from you for a moment, but with everlasting kindness I will have compassion on you" (Isa 54:8).

Amen! The terms of the Lord's love for His people are unconditional. His covenant is not predicated upon Israel's behavior; it's predicated on Yahweh's compassion—immovable, unshakable, relentless compassion. Isaiah's words are truer today than they ever were. Even if the mountains of world opinion, and the hills of popular theology, shake and shift all around that tiny nation, the Lord's steadfast love remains. And one day, that love will prevail in Jesus' name. All Israel will be saved. God has a heart for Israel.

CHAPTER 4

GOD'S HISTORIC LOVE FOR HIS PEOPLE: THE NEW TESTAMENT

JESUS' HEART FOR ISRAEL

When we read Old Testament passages like those in the last chapter, we are confronted by God's great heart for Israel. Any personal preferences or prejudices must take a back seat to God's Word. His love for Israel is eternal and His plan for them will come to pass.

But if those words from the Hebrew Bible were not enough to convince us, Jesus seals the deal. The same Lord who spoke through the prophets and kings has since come to Israel in the flesh. Rabbi Yeshua from Nazareth was none other than Yahweh in person. When He visited His people, He powerfully confirmed God's promises and heart for Israel.

God's covenant with Israel is not just an "Old Testament thing." It's a "New Testament thing." In fact, it's a Jesus thing! So I encourage you to read these quotes from Jesus with the same open, prayerful heart as you did the last chapter. Listen closely to the way Jesus revealed "God's Heart for Israel."

I was sent only to the lost sheep of the house of Israel (Matt 15:24).

"Lost sheep" may not sound like a striking term. It's such a familiar biblical image that we can read through it without much thought. There are few passages in the Bible more familiar than the twenty-third psalm: "The Lord is my shepherd..." Scripture often refers to Israel as God's sheep (Psa 100:3). Indeed, "all of us like sheep have gone astray, each of us has turned to his own way" (Isa 53:6). So when we read that Jesus is the "Good Shepherd" (John 10:11) and Israel consists of His "lost sheep," it doesn't surprise us.

But maybe it should. When I consider the history of God's chosen people, I don't think merely of "lost sheep." I think of something far worse. The story of my people is an epic tragedy filled with rebellion and judgment. Though God delivered them from slavery and made them His own, they often repaid Him with the worst kinds of idolatry, violence, and even witchcraft.

Then they capped off their rebellion by rejecting their own Messiah, colluding with the Romans to destroy Him. When I think about this history, I don't think "lost sheep." I think of something closer to Isaiah's description: "A people whose guilt is great, a brood of evildoers, children given to corruption! They have forsaken the Lord; they have spurned the Holy One of Israel and turned their backs on him" (Isa 1:4).

GOD'S COVENANT WITH ISRAEL IS NOT JUST AN "OLD TESTAMENT THING." IT'S A "NEW TESTAMENT THING." IN FACT, IT'S A JESUS THING!

Meanwhile, the phrase "lost sheep" brings a much different image to my mind. I picture cute lambs feeding in the Judean hills. A few stroll away from the flock, wandering off as they search for an extra patch of green grass. More green over here leads to more green over there. Next thing you know, they're alone in a strange, scary place with no sign of their flock or shepherd. Poor little guys! They didn't try to wander away; they were just looking around. They're not evil. They're just lost! Right?

OK, maybe I'm overdoing it. But you get the point. "Lost sheep" just doesn't seem like an accurate way to describe Israel's dismal track record—especially when

Jesus knew they would hand Him over to be crucified. How could Jesus really call Israel "lost sheep"?

He could call them "lost sheep" because Jesus was not merely describing the history of Israel. He was describing *His heart for Israel!* No matter the conduct of Israel in the past, the Lord loved them and wanted to shepherd them back into His fold. They may have abandoned Him, but He would never abandon them. In His Good Shepherd's heart, Jesus saw that Israel was lost. But they were still His flock. So just when we might have expected Him to come and condemn them, *He came looking for them.*

If you don't share that same heart toward Israel, I encourage you to ask the Lord to download His perspective into your heart and mind.

You worship what you do not know; we worship what we know, for salvation is from the Jews (John 4:22).

Like the previous verse, this does not seem like a striking pronouncement of Jesus' heart for Israel. It's more like a simple statement of fact. Jesus makes the comment during His conversation with the Samaritan woman. He had been carefully unveiling his identity to her, working to lead her to salvation. Compared to that lofty goal, this statement about the Jews almost sounds like a passing comment on the way to something more important. But let's look at it more closely.

Jesus actually makes two statements that powerfully express His heart for Israel.

First, Jesus refers to the Jews as "we" rather than "they." I absolutely love that. As a Jewish man, I am proud that Jesus (Yeshua) was not only a thoroughly Jewish man, but *candidly claimed His own Jewishness* without blinking. He was not ashamed to be a Jew! He clearly identified with the Jewish people.

> JESUS (YESHUA) WAS NOT ONLY A THOROUGHLY JEWISH MAN, BUT *CANDIDLY CLAIMED HIS OWN JEWISHNESS* WITHOUT BLINKING.

Even after their long history of rebellion and their soon rejection of Him as their Messiah, the Jews are not *those people*. They are *My people*. What a heart for Israel! That little English word "we" is so much more than a pronoun. It represents God's heart of grace toward Israel, and Jesus' deep, emotional, and personal solidarity with His own Jewish people.

Second, Jesus declares Israel's unique role while showing equal love toward Gentiles. Many Christians struggle with this tension. But Jesus did not. With one simple statement He maintains the special place of

Jews in God's heart and plan, while calling a Gentile into His Kingdom.

Remember what John, the Gospel writer, tells us earlier in this story: "Jews had no dealings with Samaritans" (John 4:9). This is because, in Jesus' day, Jews looked down on Samaritans. When the Jewish leaders became angry with Jesus, they called Him a "Samaritan" and said He had a demon (John 8:48). Jewish people disdained their northern neighbors as a mixed race that worshipped God the wrong way and in the wrong place.

JESUS CLEARLY DEMONSTRATES THAT GOD LOVES ALL NATIONS EQUALLY AND OFFERS ALL NATIONS HIS SALVATION.

But in this story, Jesus breaks down these cultural barriers. He was not prejudiced toward these people, though popular opinion said He should have been. Rather, He was in the process of calling this woman to be a worshipper of God "in Spirit and in truth" on equal footing with His Jewish disciples (John 4:23-24). Jesus clearly demonstrates that God loves all nations equally and offers all nations His salvation. It did not matter if they were Jews or Gentiles. All were invited to believe.

But still, when it came to Israel's unique, historical role, Jesus would not budge. God may equally love all nations, but the nation of Israel still had a special calling. The Jewish people have a distinct history and experience of God that no other nation shares. Even though God now intends that experience to spread to other nations, it does not negate the special role of Israel. God used that nation—and no other nation—to bring this knowledge to the world. Jesus both affirms and honors that. "Salvation is from the Jews." No matter how much the Jews failed in the past, Jesus esteems them for their calling to bring God's Messiah, and therefore redemption, to the world.

Jerusalem, Jerusalem, who kills the prophets and stones those who are sent to her! How often I wanted to gather your children together, the way a hen gathers her chicks under her wings, and you were unwilling (Matt 23:37).

One of the most painful things I've experienced as a pastor was the despair of a mother whose adult child wanted nothing to do with her. Anguish pained her face and voice as she explained that, not only was she alienated from her own child, but also from her grandchildren. The ache in her heart led to many sleepless nights as she wondered how to reconnect with her

JESUS WAS NOT A CHRISTIAN

child. No matter how often she attempted to reach out, the child refused. Her grief was palpable. I don't think I could ever bear it.

THOUGH JUDGMENT IS NECESSARY, THE HEART OF THE MESSIAH BLEEDS WITH LOVE AND MERCY FOR HIS PEOPLE.

Only a mother can understand the unique bond she shares with her children. So only a mother can understand the unique pain of alienation from her children. I believe this is one of the few places in Scripture where Jesus uses a feminine image for Himself. He does not refer to a macho rooster, but rather a sensitive hen. Only a maternal figure could portray the intense pain Jesus feels because of His estranged people.

What a surprising image Jesus used. We might expect Him to say something like, "I want to destroy this rebellious, murderous city!" But can you imagine a mother's reacting to her estranged children that way? No one denies that wrongs were committed, but a mother's heart will always want her children back. Her longing for reconnection will outrun her anger. Likewise, Jesus did not deny Jerusalem's unholy history. He even confronted it. But that's just what makes Jesus' words of compassion so amazing. They come from a heart that resembles a mother's heart, not an enemy's heart.

Though judgment is necessary, the *heart* of the Messiah bleeds with love and mercy for His people. Just when we think He has every right to express frustration, He expresses love and loyalty. He longs to show Jerusalem His tender—even maternal—heart of compassion, and to bring its people back to Himself. Yes, judgment is coming. But Jesus' *heart* is not to destroy His people. His heart is to regather them. No wonder His closing statement declared that, one day, the leaders of this wayward city would shout to Jesus, "Blessed is He who comes in the name of the Lord!" (Matt 23:39). His heart's desire will one day be fulfilled!

Yes, Lord! We want the same heart—the *Messiah's* heart—for Israel, and we pray for their salvation.

PAUL'S HEART FOR ISRAEL

Paul was a Jew, but Jesus called him to be an "apostle to the Gentiles." That means he was a special emissary from God to bring the Good News of the Jewish Messiah to the many ethnic groups around the world. His ministry was a great example of Israel's historic calling to be a light to the nations. So Paul traveled extensively throughout the Roman Empire. His mission took him from Syria, just north of Israel, all the way around the Mediterranean Sea to Italy, and then even to Spain. Paul was indeed the Jewish "apostle to the Gentiles."

But Paul's emphasis on the Gentiles did not take away his heart for Israel. Whatever Roman city he entered, he always visited the Jewish synagogue first. He gave priority to the Jewish people though his main call was to the Gentiles. So as God invited Gentiles everywhere to believe in Jesus, Paul knew God's love and plan for Israel remained.

> *I speak the truth in Christ—I am not lying, my conscience confirms it through the Holy Spirit—I have great sorrow and unceasing anguish in my heart. For I could wish that I myself were cursed and cut off from Christ for the sake of my people, those of my own race, the people of Israel. Theirs is the adoption to sonship; theirs the divine glory, the covenants, the receiving of the law, the temple worship and the promises. Theirs are the patriarchs, and from them is traced the human ancestry of the Messiah, who is God over all, forever praised! Amen (Rom 9:1-5, NIV).*

It would be difficult to find a more poignant expression of God's heart for Israel than these words of Paul. They combine two eternal truths that flow like streams into one river. The first is God's passion *for* Israel. The second is God's call *on* Israel.

First, notice how Paul reflects God's passion for Israel by expressing his own. Consider that, once Paul became a missionary apostle, in city after city, most of his own Jewish people rejected his ministry. They often resisted and harshly persecuted him for proclaiming their Messiah to them.

> THE SAME PAUL WHO TOLD BELIEVERS ALWAYS TO REJOICE ALSO MOURNED CONTINUALLY FOR THE LOST STATE OF HIS PEOPLE.

Meanwhile, Paul found tremendous success in his Gospel ministry among those *outside* the ethnic borders of Israel.

Yet, much like Jesus, Paul does not react in anger against his beloved relatives. He does not reject the Jews, ignore them, or devise a theology that "replaces" them. Instead, *he grieves for them*. The apostle's heart was broken for his people like someone who grieved the loss of a loved one. The same Paul who told believers always to rejoice (Phil 4:4) also mourned continually for the lost state of his people (Rom 9:2). His heart was so blended with God's heart that he could both be glad in the Holy Spirit and lament for his people. Paul could even declare that, if his own separation from

Messiah could somehow bring his kinsmen to faith, he would do it.

Imagine that! Just a few verses earlier, Paul declared he was convinced *nothing* could separate us from God's love in Messiah (Rom 8:38-39). Then in the next breath, Paul proclaimed that he could wish himself cut off from the Messiah if it meant his Jewish kinsmen would know the Messiah. How could he say such a thing? Because Paul *loved* the Jewish people. His love for Israel was not a temporary sentiment that rose and fell with the way they treated him. It was a passion that ran deep into the core of his being. It was a part of who he was. When someone you love deeply is in danger or trouble, you do not merely get angry with him. You ache for him and do what you can to help him.

Paul's love drove him to action for his. He prayed continually for their salvation (Rom 10:1). He shared the Gospel with them (Acts 17:1-3). He supported poor Jewish believers in Israel (Rom 15:25-26; 1 Cor 16:1-3). He magnified his Gentile ministry to make them jealous (Rom 11:13-14). And he desperately wished he could do something more—even the impossible—to influence his compatriots toward their Messiah (Rom 9:3).

That is not the heart of someone who reacts to Jewish opposition by carrying offense, blaming them for the world's problems, or suggesting the Church has replaced them. It is rather the heart of someone who shares *God's* heart for Israel. I believe that is why Paul could discern that God's plan for Israel continued in his day. His heart was not moved by Jewish rejection of the Messiah; it was moved by God's promises. How else could he continue to hope for and proclaim Israel's future salvation (Rom 11:26)? Paul's love for Israel helped him to see past Israel's rebellion and declare their scriptural destiny.

> **PAUL'S LOVE FOR ISRAEL HELPED HIM TO SEE PAST ISRAEL'S REBELLION AND DECLARE THEIR SCRIPTURAL DESTINY.**

Which brings us to our second consideration: Paul's view of Israel's calling. In the verses quoted above, Paul gave a list of blessings God graciously invested into Israel. It is hard to exaggerate the extraordinary calling these blessings represent. They are like golden medals of honor pinned to the coat of an ambassador, indicating authority and power to represent a king. Paul was saying that, whatever would qualify a nation to be God's representative in the world, that is what qualified Israel. No other nation received such honors.

No wonder Paul loved Israel so much! He was very proud of his people. Just look at the list. What other nation did God adopt and call His "son" (see Exod

4:22-23 and Hos 11:1)? God Himself created Israel through the "patriarchs," and pledged Himself to them forever with "covenants." Only Israel boasted the "temple" as a replica of heaven on earth, which is also where they had fellowship with the "divine glory" through the "worship" prescribed in God's "Law." And if that weren't enough, God sent His eternal Son, Jesus the Messiah, into the world through Israel.

GOD STILL HAS A CALLING ON ISRAEL. HE STILL HAS A HEART FOR ISRAEL. SO SHOULD WE.

But Paul does not recount these things to say Israel is better than everyone else. Certainly not! His point is that God chose Israel to *serve* the other nations. That is why Scripture speaks of Israel as Yahweh's "servant" (Isa 41:8; 44:2, 21; 45:4; 49:3, 6). So yes, Israel is still special. And yes, Israel is still chosen. Israel has a distinctive place in God's heart and history. But the reason for that is to *be a blessing to the whole world* (Gen 12:3; 22:18; 26:4; 28:14).

That is why Paul affirmed his own, urgent love for Israel. God still has a calling on Israel. He still has a heart for Israel.

So should we.

CHAPTER 5

OUR COVENANT-
KEEPING GOD

The Bible could not be any clearer. Both Old and New Testaments declare it without question, and without apology.

God has made an everlasting covenant with Israel.

His special relationship with that nation abides forever. The same Lord who saves our souls by faith, and now gathers all believers into His Church, still intends to keep the promises He made to Abraham's natural children many centuries ago.

Listen to Jeremiah's amazing words. "Thus says the LORD, who gives the sun for light by day and the fixed order of the moon and the stars for light by night… 'If this fixed order departs from before me,' declares the LORD, 'then shall the offspring of Israel cease from being a nation before me forever.' Thus says the LORD: 'If the heavens above can be measured, and the foundations of the earth below can be explored, then I will cast off all the offspring of Israel for all that they have done,' declares the LORD" (Jer 31:35-37).

In other words, it will never happen. When God makes a covenant, He keeps it as long as the sun and stars are shining and the planets remain in orbit.

GOD MADE A COVENANT. NO MATTER HOW LONG AGO HE MADE IT, HE INTENDS TO KEEP IT.

In the New Testament, Paul's words carry the same extreme clarity: "All Israel will be saved. Just as it is written, 'The deliverer will come from Zion, He will remove ungodliness from Jacob. This is my covenant with them, when I take away their sins.' From the standpoint of the Gospel they are enemies for your sake, but from the standpoint of God's choice they are beloved for the sake of the fathers; for the gifts and the calling of God are irrevocable" (Rom 11:26-29).

God made a covenant. No matter how long ago He made it, He intends to keep it.

Does this mean that the nation of Israel is automatically saved, or that every Jew is saved just because he or she is a Jew? Of course not. All have sinned. All need atonement—both Jews and Gentiles—and all find salvation only through faith in the Lord Jesus Christ. But the everlasting covenant God made with Israel *does* mean that, one day, Israel will turn from its sins and embrace Yeshua as their Messiah. For God's covenant with Abraham to be fulfilled, it must happen.

It will happen.

The Gospel does not negate this ancient covenant. It rather guarantees its fulfillment. "For I say that Christ became a servant of the circumcised on behalf of God's truth, *to confirm the promises to the fathers*, and so that Gentiles may glorify God for his mercy" (Rom 15:8-9).

Did you see that? The Messiah did not negate God's covenant promises to Abraham, Isaac, and Jacob. He *confirmed* them! He did not transfer those promises to the Gentiles. Instead, the Messiah's New Covenant affirmed the original covenant and then welcomed people from all nations to be included. But the ancient covenant with Abraham's children remains intact and will be fulfilled. Our God keeps His covenant.

This is why Paul could boldly declare, "All Israel shall be saved!" Can these words be any clearer? One day will come a massive, Messianic revival among Jews throughout the world! Israel *as a nation* will believe in its only true King, positioning itself to receive every promise rooted in God's covenant with Abraham. They will possess their land, experience all of God's blessings, enjoy national greatness and honor, and be a blessing to the world. All of this will be fulfilled in the Messiah Yeshua.

But if this is so clear, why do so many in the Church doubt it? Why do some believe God's promises to Israel now only apply spiritually to the Church? Why has much of the Church cut itself off from its Jewish roots? Why have so many Christians ignored Israel's special place in God's plan—or the burden in God's heart—as peripheral at best or irrelevant at worst?

One reason is that the devil works hard to blind the Church to Israel's role in God's plan. Another reason is the pervasive anti-Semitism that has gripped our world and overflowed into the Church. But the reason on which I focus here is this: *Too many Christians have a low view of "covenant."*

GOD'S COVENANT NATURE

If we understood what a covenant really is—and particularly, what a covenant flowing out of God's covenantal nature is—we would acknowledge God's enduring commitment to the nation of Israel and share His burden. We would honor it in our hearts, teach about it in our churches, and pray about it with tears.

A covenant is a permanent bond—a pledge of heart, mind, and body. If God made a covenant with Abraham, then that's that. It stands forever. No matter what our personal views of Israel's current positions or policies, we should still honor God's words the same way He does. We must let His promises take precedence over our political or emotional hang-ups.

Even if most Jews today are unsaved, and even if at times they are "enemies from the Gospel's standpoint," they are also "beloved because of the fathers." The international family of Christ should honor the Lord's bond with Israel and long for its firstborn brother to return to the fold.

> A COVENANT IS A PERMANENT BOND—A PLEDGE OF HEART, MIND, AND BODY.

Do we really think God would make promises to Israel, in clear, covenantal oaths, and later change them to mean something else? Would He really make vows to Abraham's children and them leave them in the dust? To God, covenant is not a flexible or adjustable contract. It is a once-for-all constant—an expression of the deepest kind of love and highest kind of integrity. Once made, it lasts forever. That's just who God is—the ultimate keeper of His Word.

When the Bible says, "God is love," it means love permeates His entire essence the way flames permeate fire. God inherently burns throughout His eternal being with a passionate longing to share Himself with His children, give them life, bless them, serve them, and remain loyal to them forever. He cannot love any other way.

So when God loves, He loves "covenantally"—and only covenantally. His kind of love cannot and will not transfer on a whim or even turn on the actions of His children. When He loves, it is only natural for Him to commit Himself forever to His beloved. It does not make sense to God's heart to love only up to a point. His love is without limit, and therefore must translate into loyalty without limit. In other words, to say "God is love" is to say, "God is covenantal."

My wife and I absolutely love our children. When each of them was born, we did not have to take an oath to say we would take care of them. That was automatic. The bond came from deep in our hearts. It was natural. Even when they are grown and married, though we are no longer responsible for them in the same way, and they are no longer under our household authority, we would still do anything we could to help and support them. Nothing will ever break that bond.

Can you imagine our disowning them because they argued, broke rules, or even defied us? I'm thankful we have great kids and didn't have to deal with any real rebellion. But what if one of them did go astray? Or went through a period when he or she constantly breached our trust? Even if we had to draw more boundaries and discipline them, we would never abandon them, let alone seek other children to replace them! Our natural "covenant" would never allow that.

I would never say, "Hey Buddy, you just broke curfew for the last time. You'll have to hit the curb. Now Mom and I are going to adopt one of the neighbors' kids to replace you."

"But Dad! What about all the promises you made to help me get my first job and pay for part of my tuition? Won't you keep your word?"

"Oh, I'll keep my word…by applying those promises to the new kid!"

Sounds silly, doesn't it? But that is how some people under-stand God's covenant with Israel. If earthly parents have such a natural bond with their children, how much more will God bind Himself to His! But you know what? Beth and I never made an explicit oath to our children. We never drew up a parental contract of love promising we would provide this much comfort or that many meals. Our covenant with them was organic, written on our hearts before they were even born.

God, on the other hand, has a much more natural, covenantal love for His children. His loyalty is more pure and His promises more sure than even our love for our children. He would need an explicit covenant

IF EARTHLY PARENTS HAVE SUCH A NATURAL BOND WITH THEIR CHILDREN, HOW MUCH MORE WILL GOD BIND HIMSELF TO HIS!

far less than we would. *But He still made that covenant with His chosen people.* Though every word He speaks is already the purist gold—as pure and eternal as the love from which it comes—He still made a specific covenant to assure His people He would remain loyal to them forever.

"For when God made a promise to Abraham, since he had no one greater to swear by, he swore by himself: I will indeed bless you, and I will greatly multiply you. And so, after waiting patiently, Abraham obtained the promise. For people swear by something greater than themselves, and for them a confirming oath ends every dispute. Because God wanted to show his unchangeable purpose even more clearly to the heirs of the promise, he guaranteed it with an oath, so that through two unchangeable things, in which it is impossible for God to lie, we who have fled for refuge might have strong encouragement to seize the hope set before us" (Heb 6:13-18).

A WORLD OF BROKEN PROMISES

How could we doubt God's historic, covenantal promises to Israel? I believe it is because we live in a world that does not keep its word. We have adopted its standards and projected them on to God. Even among believers, our words can mean very little. The divorce rate among Christians is often as high as the divorce rate in the world. Further, our paradigm for "Church" has all but forsaken any idea of covenant.

We have become far less of a family and far more of a customer base that chooses the church that best "meets our needs." Rather than feeling the covenantal bond

WE LIVE IN A FAMINE OF COVENANT.

of family members, sharing life and serving one another as real brothers and sisters, we have become consumers seeking products. We treat churches like they are spiritual businesses, not families. If we do not get our money's or time's worth, we simply attend somewhere else. Where is the covenant in that? Can we even imagine "church" defined as a family rather than a ministry agency, building, staff, and head pastor? Don't think this is a minor issue. Many believers have all but lost their loving sense of covenant.

Why, then, should we expect God to be covenantal? By our standards, we should *expect* Him to switch allegiances. Israel disappointed God, so He left them to attend the Gentile Church! It sounds absurd, really, but this is basically the way many people think. We live in a famine of covenant. If God is truly a covenant-keeping God, that implies we should be a covenant-keeping people. But if we really don't want to live a covenantal life, then we must adjust our view of God's covenantal character too.

Think about the culture we are tempted to reflect. Word commitments mean little. Hollywood entertainers get married many times—each time promising permanent devotion. Business deals are constantly broken. In sports, contracts are rarely guaranteed. (But isn't that the whole point of a "contract"?) One coach signed twenty-five years' worth of contracts with four different teams during a seven-year period! How is that even possible? Don't words mean anything?

What about marriage vows? We have prenuptial agreements and no-fault divorces because our society expects people to break their promises, and even to a degree accommodates this lack of integrity. We have become experts at breaking our promises, and then experts at legally protecting ourselves so that we *can* break our promises. Yet God created us in His image. He designed our ability to speak so that our words come purely and directly from our hearts. Like God, our words are meant to reflect our very souls. Instead, we actually use our words deceitfully to serve our own interests.

Is it any wonder we project that same code of dishonor on God? But God is the opposite of that. When He speaks His Word, He invests His whole being into what He says. Love to Him is an eternal vow. To go back on that would be to contradict His nature. "God is light and in Him there is no darkness at all" (1 John 1:5). The thought of going back on a promise does not compute with Him. The idea is abhorrent, and even silly. God simply does not talk that way. Ever. God is love—a covenant-keeping God.

THE RADICAL ABRAHAMIC COVENANT

That is why, throughout Scripture, God made covenants with His people. He wanted to give His love and loyalty the ultimate expressions, holding Himself to oaths. Not that He needed to be held accountable. But He wanted to give His people assurance—set in the stones of unmistakable, unbreakable commitments—that He loved them and would care for them in various ways. God promised Noah, for example, He would never again destroy the earth with a flood of water (Gen 9). In the Mosaic covenant, God promised Israel distinction as His people, national identity, security, and multiplied blessings in their own Land if they would obey His Law (Exod 19). God also made a covenant with David that guaranteed one of his sons would rule Israel forever (2 Sam 7).

But God's covenant with Abraham is our special focus. That covenant guarantees Israel would never lose its identity as God's special nation with its own Land. The Mosaic covenant was conditional. It promised blessings on obedience and curses on disobedience. God's treatment was contingent on Israel's behavior. If they disobeyed the Lord's commands, they would suffer and be exiled from their Land. And that happened. But the Abrahamic covenant was unconditional—and eternal.

A careful reading of the ritual between Yahweh and Abraham makes this clear. The remarkable ceremony between God and His man was not for decoration. It was an indescribably sacred act of covenant that committed Yahweh to Abraham's children forever. In the following sequence, the Lord of heaven and earth "burned His ships at the shore," so to speak, surrendering His love to Abraham's children forever.

> "[The LORD] took [Abram] outside and said, 'Look at the sky and count the stars, if you are able to count them.' Then he said to him, 'Your offspring will be that numerous.' Abram believed the Lord, and he credited it to him as righteousness. He also said to him, 'I am the Lord who brought you from Ur of the Chaldeans to give you this Land to possess.' But he said, 'Lord God, how can I know that I will possess it?' He said to him, 'Bring me a three-year-old cow,

a three-year-old female goat, a three-year-old ram, a turtledove, and a young pigeon.' So he brought all these to him, cut them in half, and laid the pieces opposite each other, but he did not cut the birds in half. Birds of prey came down on the carcasses, but Abram drove them away. As the sun was setting, a deep sleep came over Abram, and suddenly great terror and darkness descended on him… When the sun had set and it was dark, a smoking fire pot and a flaming torch appeared and passed between the divided animals. On that day the Lord made a covenant with Abram, saying, 'I give this Land to your offspring, from the brook of Egypt to the great river, the Euphrates River…' " (Gen 15, CSB).

What a story! It's like a chest full of too many treasures to grasp. So here we will focus on a few points to illustrate the nature of God's covenant with Israel. First, this covenant is *unilateral*. That means it's one-sided. Yahweh took the initiative and presented a pact already put together. He simply stepped into Abram's life and started telling him all He would do. In fact, the ritual described above actually confirms promises Yahweh gave Abram earlier in Gen 12:1-3. Each promise begins with one decisive phrase: *"I will…*

- Make you a great nation.
- Bless you.
- Make your name great.
- Make you a blessing.
- Bless those who bless you.
- Curse those who curse you.
- Bless all the families in the earth through you."

Nowhere does Yahweh say, "So Abram, do you have any ideas or preferences for this covenant? I'm open to suggestions! This is a pretty major deal; I need your input. Maybe you should take a few months and think about it. Talk it over with Sarai. Pray about it. Let me know what works for you and perhaps we can work out an agreement that works for both of us."

No. God made this covenant without input from Abraham or anyone else. It was a totally lopsided proposition. God put it forward on His terms, and made Abraham an offer of love, honor, and significance he could not refuse. It was all on God; He would do it all. When He says, "I will," He means, "I will."

Which leads to our second point. This covenant is *unconditional*. Abraham may not have had negotiating power, but neither did he have conditions to fulfill. God alone swore His commitment to Abraham. No requirement of Abraham was necessary. This is why Yahweh performed such a strange but powerful covenant ceremony. Unlike the Mosaic covenant, Yahweh obligated only Himself to keep the covenant promises.

The main promise addressed in this passage was the Land of Canaan—a Land that currently belonged to at least ten other nations (Gen 15:19-21)! Meanwhile, Abraham's family had not yet reached "multiplied like the stars of heaven" status. So he begged for assurance, and Yahweh responded immediately. He gave Abraham instructions to sacrifice animals into two pieces opposite each other.

Then the strangest thing happened. Abraham fell into a deep sleep as the sun was setting. But this was no pleasant sleep. Terror and darkness settled on him, sinking him into a supernatural stupor for divine purpose. And that is just when Yahweh arrived. Amid the darkness and terror, Yahweh came to the sacred, ceremonial site to bind Himself to Abraham and his children forever. He appeared as a smoking oven and a burning torch—forms that embodied His faithful presence during the Exodus—and passed through the pieces of sacrificial flesh all by Himself.

Often in the ancient world, when two parties made a covenant, they both would pass between slaughtered animal parts while reciting their mutual obligations. It was a way of saying, "If I don't keep my end of the covenant, then let what happened to these animals happen to me!" But in the case with Abraham, only the Lord walked through the pieces...*while Abraham slept*.

Do you see the picture? Only one party passed through the animal parts. Only God recited conditions He had to keep. Only God bound Himself to an oath: He would multiply Abraham's descendants and indeed bring them into this Land—all while Abraham slept. God could not have given a more graphic display of His unconditional covenant.

Finally, therefore, this covenant is *eternal*. What else could it be? If God is the covenant-keeping God who cut a unilateral and unconditional covenant with Abraham and his descendants, how could such a covenant possibly have an expiration date? It does not depend on the people's faithfulness. It depends on God's faithfulness! By virtue of God's very nature, His covenant with Abraham—with all of its promises of national identity, blessing, and Land—must abide forever. Israel may suffer temporary exile because of its sins. It may experience even extreme judgment. But in the end, God's eternal promises will come to pass.

> "I will establish my covenant as an *everlasting* covenant between me and you and your descendants after you for the generations to come, to be your God and the God of your descendants

after you. The whole land of Canaan, where you now reside as a foreigner, I will give as an *everlasting* possession to you and your descendants after you; and I will be their God" (Gen 17:7-8, NIV).

"He remembers his covenant *forever*, the promise he made, for a thousand generations, the covenant he made with Abraham, the oath he swore to Isaac. He confirmed it to Jacob as a decree, to Israel as an *everlasting* covenant: To you I will give the land of Canaan as the portion you will inherit" (Psa 105:8-11, NIV).

"I will make a covenant of peace with them; it will be an *everlasting* covenant. I will establish them and increase their numbers, and I will put my sanctuary among them *forever*" (Ezek 37:26, NIV).

OUR RESPONSE

At the core of our convictions, we must recover a vision of God as the covenant-keeping God. From Abraham to Messiah, God's love compels Him to enter explicit, binding relationships He will never forsake. But what does all this imply for us?

First, the Church should adopt God's commitment to Israel as our own commitment to Israel. We should grieve for the lost sheep of the house of Israel, pray for their salvation, evangelize them, and teach fellow believers to do the same. (More on this in the last chapter.)

THE CHURCH SHOULD ADOPT GOD'S COMMITMENT TO ISRAEL AS OUR OWN COMMITMENT TO ISRAEL.

The hearts of apostolic Christians should say with Paul: "Brethren, my heart's desire and my prayer to God for them is for their salvation" (Rom 10:1). But we pray this, not merely because we feel sorry for lost Jews, but because we long for God's covenant with them to be fulfilled. The Church should see itself as God's household, a covenantal family. As such, we should long for our elder-brother nation to return to the fold and celebrate the victory of Yeshua with us!

Second, we should be people of our word. A godly lifestyle, after all, should flow out of our theology. And our theology should tell us that God is a covenant-keeping God who will keep His ancient oath to Abraham. That commitment actually implies something about our personal integrity. Through faith in Yeshua, we are in covenant with God. And covenant people should be, well, people of covenant. "Lord, who may dwell in your sanctuary? Who may live on your holy hill? He whose walk is blameless and who does what is righteous...who keeps his oath even when it hurts" (Psa 15:1-4). God keeps His Word. So should we.

Finally, let's believe God to fulfill His promises to us. God's faithfulness reaches to the heavens, but it also reaches into the details of our lives. Has He shown you that a loved one would be saved? Did He give you a vision about your life? Are there old promises you've placed on the shelf? Dust them off and believe again. If God remembers His promises to Abraham many centuries ago, He surely remembers His promises to you.

Throughout history and our lives, our God is a covenant-keeping God.

CHAPTER 6

THE GOD WHO GIVES LIFE TO THE DEAD: ISRAEL'S PAST

There is a pattern throughout Scripture we cannot ignore. It is undeniable and indisputable, like a DNA code embedded into the cells of salvation history. It holds a message of profound hope for all believers. But it especially holds a message of hope for Israel. *God raises the dead.* Over and over, this pattern appears in the Bible from creation to judgment and everywhere in between. Its sheer consistency demands our attention and inspires our faith. We must allow God's strategy of resurrection to touch our hearts. If we do not, we will fail to grasp His heart for Israel, His future intentions for Israel, and our calling into His plan for Israel.

Paul articulates this pattern to the believers in Rome. When he looks to illustrate the faith that justifies sinners, Paul appeals to Abraham as his example:

"For this reason it is by faith, in order that it may be in accordance with grace, so that the promise will be guaranteed to all the descendants, not only to those who are of the Law, but also to those who are of the faith of Abraham, who is the father of us all (as it is written, 'A father of many nations have I made you'), in the presence of Him whom he believed, even God, who gives life to the dead and calls into being that which does not exist. In hope against hope he believed, so that he might become a father of many nations according to that which had been spoken, 'So shall your descendants be.' Without becoming weak in faith he contemplated his own body, now as good as dead since he was about a hundred years old, and the deadness of Sarah's womb; yet, with respect to the promise of God, he did not waver in unbelief but grew strong in faith, giving glory to God, and being fully assured that what God had promised, He was able also to perform" (Rom 4:16-21).

Why did Paul choose Abraham as his model of faith, even for us under the New Covenant? Because Abraham exercised the one kind of faith that makes a person righteous. It is the faith that believes God is the God *who gives life to the dead and calls into being that which does not exist.* That is the only faith worthy of Abraham's God, and it is the only faith that saves (Rom 10:9-10). God gave Abraham promises that were humanly impossible to fulfill. But the father of faith was not deterred. If his God could create all things out of nothing, then He could also resurrect the dead!

Abraham dared to believe that his God was like no god worshipped by the other nations. The God of Abraham was not a god limited to the imaginations of mere mortals. He was not a god that had to use terror and manipulation to get people to serve him. He was, rather, a living God who promised blessing and gave life! So as God continued to give Abraham promises that contradicted natural circumstances, Abraham came to believe that this God had a unique ability: He could even overcome the finality of death itself. What other "god" could do such a thing? This God could reach beyond the grave—where no one else could reach—and bring the dead back to life. Yes, Abraham learned that this God who created all things out of nothing could do the same for him.

Think about this. God is in the business of taking what is nothing and turning it into something. He's in the business of taking what is dead and reviving it into life. When the Father raised Jesus from the dead, He simply did what comes naturally to Him. He demonstrated His essential character and the consistent pattern in all His dealings. God grants life where

GOD IS IN THE BUSINESS OF TAKING WHAT IS NOTHING AND TURNING IT INTO SOMETHING.

is no life. It's His favorite thing to do.

As we will see, this pattern of death-to-resurrection so persists throughout Scripture that it has an unavoidable application to Israel. No matter how many times they fell into sin...no matter how many nations tried to wipe them out...no matter how much they continue to reject their own Messiah...no matter how hardened and far gone they seem...God will surely fulfill His promises to them. How could He not?

He is the God who raises the dead.

THE CREATION OF THE WORLD

We see this resurrection pattern from the first moment of history. "In the beginning God created the heavens and the earth. The earth was *formless and void*... Then God said..." (Gen 1:1-3, emphasis mine). And from that point, a bleak, chaotic, watery darkness began to explode with light, earth, vegetation, trees, fruit, sun, moon, stars, days, seasons, fish, birds, beasts, and finally humans to take care of it all. Where there was gloom, disorder, and death, there was now color, order, and life.

So when Genesis says the earth was "formless and void," it sets the resurrection pattern into motion. That simple phrase serves as the beginning of the scriptural theme: God takes something meaningless in itself and turns it into something awe inspiring and beautiful. In other words, *"He speaks into being that which does not exist."* And everything He creates is good!

It's staggering to consider that God created the galaxies out of nothing. He determined the number of the stars, and calls each by name (Psa 147:4). A simple Google search will tell you that there are somewhere between 100 and 400 billion stars in the Milky Way galaxy alone. But that's not all. There are at least 100 billion galaxies in the observable universe! That means there could be as many as 40 sextillion stars out there! (Which, written out, would be 40,000,000,000,000,000,000,000 stars.) That's a lot of stars, and a lot of names for God to remember.

Where there used to be a formless void, God stepped in and spoke, making an environment so vast, complex, and vibrant that we can hardly begin to wrap our brains around it. Most of our ocean depths are still unexplored; most matter and energy in space remain unidentified. Yet Job tells us that "these are but the fringes of His ways, and how faint is the word we hear of Him!" (Job 26:14). The immense mystery of creation declares it. God makes everything out of nothing and brings life out of death.

THE CREATION OF MAN

Then it happened again. After hurling hundreds of billions of stars into space (and naming them), placing the sun and moon in their orbits, and carving out the continents, God does something different with man. Rather than "speaking" him into existence, He forms him out of the dust of the earth and breathes into him the breath of life (Gen 2:7)!

Dust is something we would readily sweep away as a meaningless and useless substance—a nuisance on our furniture and an irritant in our nostrils. But God takes it into His hands, shapes it into something "fearfully and wonderfully made," and breathes life into it from *His* nostrils. You can't get more "dead" than dust. Yet when God stared into dust's desolation, He saw value and glory. What used to be lifeless dirt, the Lord molded into His very image and infused with His very breath. Few images carry the pattern of "life from the dead" with greater force.

But there's even more. Not only is "dust" something completely useless without God's creativity and life, but it's also the place the dead are buried. Look carefully at the picture Genesis paints: "Then the Lord God formed a man from the dust of the ground and breathed into his nostrils the breath of life, and the man became a living being" (Gen 2:7). Do you see the resurrection pattern? God shaped the man *from the ground.* Adam came out of the earth as a kind of prelife grave, and then received divine breath to live.

JUST AS THE FIRST ADAM CAME FROM THE GROUND, SO DID THE "LAST ADAM"—AND SO DO ALL OF US WHO FOLLOW HIM.

When the Father raised Jesus from the dead, He took Him from the ground where He was buried (1 Cor 15:4). He "raised" Adam from the same place where the dead are buried. It's the same pattern when new disciples are baptized in water. They go down into a burial and rise to "newness of life" (Rom 6:3-4). They are a "new creation." Just as the first Adam came from the ground, so did the "last Adam"—and so do all of us who follow Him. Then one day all the dead in Messiah will rise from the dust with glorified bodies (1 Cor 15:20-49). Life from the dead! Creation is an act of resurrection; resurrection is an act of creation. The pattern is consistent and undeniable.

THE CREATION OF ISRAEL

The same pattern continued with the creation of Israel and the Jewish people. God called a man named Abram from the lineage of Shem (the Semites). Abram would be the father of a new nation on earth, and a new era in history. But notice the inauspicious way Abram's call to nationhood began:

"Terah lived seventy years, and became the father of Abram, Nahor and Haran...Abram and Nahor took wives for themselves. The name of Abram's wife was Sarai [later named Sarah]...*Sarai was barren; she had no child*" (Gen 11:26-30).

Each time I read this verse it feels like a sucker punch to the stomach. It takes my breath away. God is about to make Abram the father of a great nation that is called to bless all the other nations of the earth. Yet He allows Abram to choose a wife whose womb is dead! As an earthly father, I would have done everything I could to steer Abram to a woman who would be able to carry his children and guarantee the family name would continue.

But our heavenly Father is altogether different. Just as He was glorified through a formless, empty universe and some useless dust, so He will be glorified through the deadness of Sarah's womb. The basis for the Lord's choices has nothing to do with human abilities. Indeed,

He looks for people who recognize their own inabilities so He may be glorified through them. His way of choosing is altogether different than man's way of choosing.

"God chose the weak things of the world to shame the strong. God chose the...things that are not to nullify the things that are, so that no one may boast before Him... Therefore, as it is written: 'Let the one who boasts boast in the Lord' " (1 Cor 1:27-31, NIV).

God chooses frail humans, strapped by impossibilities, to humble our pride while displaying His glory. This is precisely why He commands us to consider the story of Abraham and Sarah. It tells us something crucial about Israel's history, as well as its future.

> GOD CHOOSES FRAIL HUMANS, STRAPPED BY IMPOSSIBILITIES, TO HUMBLE OUR PRIDE WHILE DISPLAYING HIS GLORY.

"Listen to me, you who pursue righteousness and who seek the Lord: Look to the rock from which you were cut and the quarry from which you were hewn; *look to Abraham, your father, and to Sarah who gave you birth.* When I called him he was only one man, and I blessed him and made him many" (Is 51:1-3, NIV).

The Abraham and Sarah story reverberates with the same death-to-life pattern found throughout

Scripture. Rather than making His promise to a young, fertile couple, God waits until Sarah is "beyond the age of bearing children" (Gen 18:11; Heb 11:11) and Abraham's body is "as good as dead" (Rom 4:19). Sarah was barren anyway. But at this point she was also past menopause. That means no one could attribute her pregnancy to a natural change in her body. She was past that stage. Meanwhile Abraham was nearly one hundred years old. That means his ability to father a child was as good as dead! From the human perspective, there's no chance life will ever come out of this union. But from the divine perspective, this union creates the perfect equation for God's supernatural solution to be on full display.

The name "Abram" means "exalted father." Yet he lived the majority of his life without children. When the Lord changed his name to "Abraham," literally the "father of multitudes," he was already 99 years old and still had no children! Abraham lived with a name that defied his natural reality. His name and real-life situation were diametrically opposed to each other. Yet the Lord had a plan to do something for him and Sarah that would demonstrate life from the dead.

"Then the Lord took note of Sarah as He had said and the Lord did for Sarah as He had promised. So Sarah conceived and bore a son to Abraham in his old age, at the appointed time of which God had spoken to him" (Gen 21:1-2).

The Lord has fixed an *appointed time* to fulfill His promises. Although such an appointed time may not fit into our time schedule, it certainly fits into His! Just as there was an appointed time for Abraham and Sarah to conceive, so also there is an appointed time for Israel's salvation. And that moment, as the Bible calls it, will be "life from the dead" (Rom 11:15).

THE GOD WHO REFERS TO HIMSELF AS "THE GOD OF ABRAHAM, ISAAC, AND JACOB" ALSO IDENTIFIES HIMSELF AS "THE GOD WHO GIVES LIFE TO THE DEAD."

God's covenant with Abraham passed to his son Isaac, and to Isaac's son Jacob. But so did Abraham's legacy of "life from the dead" pass on. Each of the patriarchs married barren women. Just like Sarah, both Rebekah and Rachel needed God's intervention to conceive the children of promise. Not one of the first three families God called to create "Israel" could conceive children. The God who refers to Himself as "the God of Abraham, Isaac, and Jacob" also identifies Himself as "the God who gives life to the dead." He brought life out of barrenness. Indeed, He brought an entire nation out of barrenness. Israel's initial lineage, and therefore its very essence, loudly proclaims that God is the God "who gives life to the dead, and speaks into being that which does not exist."

THE EXODUS

The Exodus from Egypt was yet another "dead raising" in Israel's history. God's people would not exist as a nation had He not given them "life" out of the "death" of slavery. When He first made covenant with Abram, the Lord told him, "Know for certain that for four hundred years your descendants will be strangers in a country not their own and that they will be enslaved and mistreated there. But I will punish the nation they serve as slaves, and afterward they will come out with great possessions (Gen 15:13-14). In other words, "Your people will go down into a grave. But I will raise them from that grave with new life!"

The tyranny, oppression, and paganism of Egypt created a tomb around the Hebrew people. God called Moses to deliver them out of that tomb. But Pharaoh refused to let God's people go. As a nation, God's people were as good as dead. They had no natural power—no political authority nor military strength—to make their own escape. They were at the mercy of a powerful empire that both feared and hated them. There was no hope outside of God's dead-raising power.

If we look closely at the Exodus story, we see that familiar pattern of life-from-the-dead. The ten plagues ravaged Egypt, culminating with the death of every firstborn. Meanwhile, the angel of death "passed over" the Hebrew families whose doors were stained with the blood of lambs. Many died for Israel's deliverance. The shadow of death covered the entire event.

But the grave gets even deeper. After Pharaoh finally let Israel go, he quickly changed his mind and pursued them to the Red Sea. Now God's people were caught in another impossible situation, "entombed" again by Pharaoh's army behind them and the sea before them. Even the people recognized the shadow of death in that moment: "Was it because there were no graves in Egypt that you brought us to the desert to die?" (Exod 14:11). That is precisely the moment God intervened with a miracle that lifted Israel out of death into life. He parted the sea, creating a path of dry land where there used to be water (Exod 14:21-22).

> WHEN GOD PARTED THE SEA AND BROUGHT ISRAEL SAFELY THROUGH, HE WAS YET AGAIN RAISING THE DEAD.

When God parted the sea and brought Israel safely through, He was yet again raising the dead. Consider the primordial image of passing through water. In

Genesis, chaotic waters covered the earth. It was dark and void of life. Before He could form the first human, God needed dry land. So He had to divide the water for dry land to appear (Gen 1:9). Then the dry land provided the raw material for God to shape the first human. Adam's creation in Genesis parallels Israel's deliverance in Exodus. In order to bring His people into life as a nation, God had to part the sea for dry land to appear. The dry land was the pathway through the chaotic waters from death to life. The Exodus was yet another resurrection for Israel.

RETURN FROM EXILE

Isaiah prophesied it would happen. So did Jeremiah. Then in 586 BC, it did happen. After many years of disobedience, sin, and idolatry, judgment came to God's people. The nation of Babylon invaded the southern kingdom of Judah. Its army destroyed Jerusalem and burned down the temple. Many of the Jewish survivors were carried as exiles into Babylon. It was an indescribable devastation. An entire book in the Bible was written just to lament the horror.

"What can I say for you? What can I compare to you, O daughter of Jerusalem? To what can I liken you so that I can comfort you, O virgin daughter of Zion? For your destruction is as vast as the sea; who can heal you?" (Lam 2:13). That's how the prophet Jeremiah described the destruction of God's own precious daughter—His nation, His treasured possession. How can Judah recover from this deathblow? This was more than exile. This was a catastrophic judgment during which the main symbols of Israel's covenant identity were wiped out.

No more temple. No more priesthood. No more sacrifices. No more Land. No more physical emblems of Torah's blessings. Instead, the one nation that belonged to the Lord, with such a deep sense of solidarity with Him and their Promised Land, was now further scattered among foreign nations. Centuries earlier, the Assyrians toppled the northern kingdom and resettled its ten tribes outside the Land. Now the southern kingdom, consisting of the last two tribes of Judah and Benjamin, was gone as well. How could there ever be an Israel again?

Ezekiel described all of this as a death. It was beyond human recovery. God's nation was gone, torn from its Land and buried among the nations. It was now a massive scattering of refugees around the world. So they either assimilated into their new surrounding cultures, or they did their best to cling to one another and maintain their identity in a wilderness of paganism. But the prophet was right. Without their homeland, exiled Israel was essentially dead.

They said of themselves, "Our bones are dried up and our hope has perished. We are completely cut off" (Ezek 37:11).

But then God spoke a word of promise. He used that language of the dead, dry, scattered bones to prophesy one of the most wonderful guarantees of Israel's final regathering and salvation. Though this passage ultimately refers to Israel's glorious future (something we will discuss in chapter 8) it also applied partially to the first return from exile. In fact, this was the original context of Ezekiel's prophecy. That modest return continued the divine pattern we see throughout Scripture. It was a mini-resurrection: "Therefore prophesy, and you must say to them, 'Thus says the Lord Yahweh: "Look! I am opening your graves, and I will bring you up from your graves, my people, and I will bring you to the Land of Israel! And you will know that I am Yahweh when I open your graves when I bring you up from your graves, my people!" ' " (Ezek 37:12-13).

So yes, the exile was the death of a nation. Foreign countries were the graves and the disjointed bones were the Jews scattered among them. But the scriptural pattern has long been established, and would touch God's people again. They cannot remain in their graves. God would keep His covenant by overcoming the finality of death itself. The prophet Jeremiah prophesied that Jews would return to their Land after a seventy-year exile (Jer 25:11; 29:10), and that is exactly what happened (2 Chron 36:20-23). The God who paved a way in the sea now released rivers in the desert. By divine intervention, small groups of Jewish exiles made their way through the wilderness and returned home. They rebuilt their altar, and eventually, their temple and city. This was a mini-resurrection—small but real.

> THE BEST IS YET TO COME. THE DEATH-TO-LIFE PATTERN CANNOT BE STOPPED; IT IS ONLY GAINING MOMENTUM.

Ezekiel's prophecy of the bones had its first, modest fulfillment when those first exiles returned home. But the best is yet to come. The death-to-life pattern cannot be stopped; it is only gaining momentum. What God began with Israel in the past, He would complete in the future.

CHAPTER 7

THE GOD WHO GIVES LIFE TO THE DEAD: ISRAEL'S PRESENT

God has proven His resurrection power throughout Israel's history. But as I said in the last chapter, the best is yet to come. It has to be! From the Babylonian exile till today, most Jews still live outside their native Land. Presently more than half of the world's Jewish population lives among the nations.

And though more Jews are coming to believe in Yeshua as their Messiah, most still do not believe. The total fulfillment of Israel's resurrection lies yet in the future. One day the whole nation will be saved and returned to its own Land. They will truly be raised from the dead! In the meantime, we live in a generation that continues to witness God's dead-raising power for Israel as a nation. What a privilege! So let's look at Israel's present state as a testimony to the God who gives life to the dead.

FROM JESUS TO MODERN TIMES

Jesus was born in Israel and lived most of His life there. (Part of His childhood was spent as a refugee in Egypt. That means even Jesus, the ultimate Jew, experienced with His people exile and *aliyah*, which means, "ascent," and refers to Jews' immigrating back to Israel.) Jesus called His disciples, performed all His miracles, died, rose from the dead, and ascended to His throne in heaven—all in Israel.

> JESUS CALLED HIS DISCIPLES, PERFORMED ALL HIS MIRACLES, DIED, ROSE FROM THE DEAD, AND ASCENDED TO HIS THRONE IN HEAVEN— ALL IN ISRAEL.

When God regathered the exiles centuries before, He was setting the stage for the coming of His Son. Israel had to exist in its Land for Jesus to fulfill His ministry. Though a province of Rome in Jesus' day, Israel still survived as a nation against the odds. The Messiah's presence in His own Land was another confirmation of Israel's history as life from the dead.

Tragically, however, Jesus "came to His own, and those who were His own did not receive Him" (John 1:11). The Jewish Messiah successfully fulfilled His mission to the world, but most of His own people rejected Him. So within a generation another "death" of Israel would occur. Yes, a remnant of Jews had believed. The very first "Church" consisted solely of Messianic Jews. It grew exponentially under persecution, and spread the Gospel throughout their Land and into the world. Praise God! But the larger nation failed to believe in its King. That rejection led to another death.

The Jewish people in the Land revolted against the Roman Empire. The Romans squashed the revolt in bloodshed and destruction. In 70 AD, the Roman army burned Jerusalem and its temple to the ground. Thousands of Jews were exiled. Six decades later, another Jewish revolt ended in another crushing defeat and another exile. This time the Roman Emperor sought to wipe out Jewish identity completely from the Land. He renamed it "Palestine," rebuilt Jerusalem under a Roman name, and erected a pagan shrine on Temple Mount. With yet another scattering throughout the nations, many Jews maintained their distinction through the study of Torah, commitment to ancestral traditions, and close community. But as a discernible nation with its own Land and sovereignty, they had died again.

For the next eighteen centuries, various nations ruled the Land of Israel. The territory God promised to Abraham, Isaac, and Jacob came under the control of Romans, Persians, Arabs, European Crusaders, Kurds, and Turks.

But in 1917, during World War I, the British Empire seized Jerusalem from the Ottoman Turkish Empire. This was another setup. God was moving history to grant His people another return from exile. By this time, Theodor Herzl, the father of modern Zionism, was already gathering Jewish leaders from around the world with the goal of establishing a nation for Jews in their homeland. Also by this time, two waves of European Jews had immigrated to the Land. Those waves hit the shores of Israel near the end of the nineteenth century ("The First Aliyah"), and at the beginning of the twentieth century ("The Second Aliyah").

They came because of persecution. They came because of economic pressure. They came because of hope. They hoped for a safe haven in a Land of their own, as well as a national identity. I believe God was the one stirring this effort. He had set into motion a "rattling of the bones"—the first divine breathings of a modern resurrection of Israel.

God was also parting the seas for His people among the nations. Before capturing Jerusalem from the Ottoman Empire, Great Britain had promised the Jews a national home in their own Land. Then with a mandate from the League of Nations, the British took official control of the Land in 1923. The promise of a modern Jewish nation in Israel was well on its way to fulfillment. But first there would be great suffering. The enemies of Israel would not sit idly by as this story unfolded. Spiritual and natural powers fought against the resurrection of Israel with all the force they possessed.

> THE HOLOCAUST WAS AN ATTEMPT TO DESTROY EVERY SINGLE JEWISH PERSON IN EUROPE—AND ULTIMATELY THE WORLD.

Yes, Zion was rising again. But so was Zion's controversy. Jewish immigration was increasing; talk of Jewish nationhood was increasing. But so was persecution against Jews in the Land. Arab inhabitants did not want to share power or territory. Surrounding nations felt the same way. There were riots and violent attacks against Jews in the Land for many years before World War II. As Hitler and the Nazis rose in power, they helped finance and arm Israel's local enemies. Even British support of Jews in the Land got weaker. Contentions against a Jewish state gathered around Israel like a dark cloud.

While God stirred Jews to return to their home-land, setting the stage for their revival as a nation, satanic forces mounted an indescribably horrible coun-terattack. The Holocaust was an attempt to destroy every single Jewish person in Europe—and ultimately the world. It was an attempt to kill and bury Israel once and for all. By God's grace, which included the fervent prayers of some Christians, the Nazis failed to reach their goal. But they did achieve the nightmare of mass murdering six million Jews. European Jewry had come close to total annihilation. It was a near death-blow to them, and to the promise of a modern state. But where the grave threatened to have the final word about Israel's existence, God once more intervened and raised His nation from the dead.

Somehow from the ashes of the Holocaust, after two thousand years of homelessness and intense perse-cution, Israel rose again. Israel became an independent nation-state for the first time since the first century BC. It declared its independence on May 14, 1948, and won its war for independence on March 10, 1949. Israel had become a sovereign nation!

If we consider the insurmountable military odds of this happening, as well as the Land's natural barren-ness at the time, it is difficult to come to any conclu-sion except that modern Israel is a miracle. God raised it from the dead. To be sure, this resurrection of statehood was not a spiritual rebirth. It was not the fulfillment of God's promises of *total* restoration—of both heart and nation. That can only happen when the Jewish people turn to Yeshua as their Messiah. But this rebirth of the political nation still testifies to God's eternal covenant with His people. The Land of Israel belongs to them, and God promised to bring them back. So after centuries of suffering banishment for their unbelief, as well as enduring the satanic attacks in the Holocaust and other persecutions, God returned His people to their homeland. There is no way this world-changing event could have occurred without God's dead-raising power.

FROM DEATH TO LIFE

From a natural point of view, Israel's national resurrection was impossible. Even some nonreligious, Jewish leaders said so. David Ben-Gurion was modern Israel's first prime minister and main founding father. He was also an agnostic. Yet he said, "In Israel, in order to be a realist you must believe in miracles."

FROM A NATURAL POINT OF VIEW, ISRAEL'S NATIONAL RESURRECTION WAS IMPOSSIBLE.

Yigael Yadin was a key leader in the Israeli army who helped design and execute its strategies for the War of Independence. Yadin was also an atheist. Yet he referred to Israel's victory in the war for independence as "The Great Miracle." When a journalist asked him how he could do this, Yadin responded,

"You are correct. I was an atheist…up until the War of Independence. There's no logical explanation for what happened."[1] Israel's victory, and sheer existence today, smacks of God's miraculous, dead-raising intervention. Consider these facts.

- The entire Arab world both inside and outside the Land stood against Israel's existence. They had already rejected the UN's partition plan of 1947. Then they promised—explicitly, publicly, and unequivocally—to attack and destroy the Jewish state the moment the last British soldier left the Land.

- Many viewed Israel's declaration of independence as a veritable suicide for the new nation. The attacking armies were much better equipped. An embargo prohibited Jews from obtaining weapons, while their enemies still obtained them easily—including some military training. The Israeli militia initially had to smuggle their weapons into Israel, or manufacture them underground.[2]

- In the years leading up to the declaration, Arabs within the Land were already attacking Jewish communities, killing many Jews. Then within hours of Israel's declaration, Syria attacked from the north. The next day four other states attacked from every side: Iraq, Egypt, Jordan, and Lebanon. The world expected Israel to be "driven into the sea."

- When the war began, Israel's enemies had hundreds of tanks, guns, and aircraft. But what about Israel's armaments? According to Israeli historian Hela Crown-Tamir, "When...five Arab countries invaded the newborn State of Israel [on May 15, 1948], it seemed her life was hanging by a thread. The new country didn't have one modern piece of artillery, not one tank, no military aircraft, few military vehicles and only 10,000 rifles for the entire defense of Israel. And those were scattered over the whole country."[3]

- Despite these uneven odds, and the grim expectations of the world, Israel had survived the first onslaught. After that the war's balance shifted. A month-long truce allowed both sides to regroup. Israel used the time to integrate thousands of new troops and weapons, and then went on the offensive. After several months of fighting, somehow, Israel had taken control of more territory than the UN's partition agreement intended to grant it. The war ended with a cease-fire in the spring of 1949. Though its enemies still refuse to acknowledge

Israel's statehood, and would continue hostilities indefinitely, God had again raised His people from the dead. Who has ever heard of such things? A nation had been brought forth in a moment (Isa 66:8).

FROM SILENCE TO SPEECH

Did you know that Modern Hebrew didn't even exist 120 years ago? After the exile in the second century, Hebrew slowly but surely faded into the nations where Jews were scattered. Many adopted the language of their new communities. Many others mixed Hebrew with German (Yiddish) or Spanish (Ladino). Here and there some Jewish communities spoke some Hebrew, but never as their main language. Ancient Hebrew was relegated to the synagogue. It became a holy language, reserved only for reading Scripture or rabbinic writings. For all intents and purposes, Hebrew as a common language was gone.

Enter a young man named Eliezer Ben-Yehuda. A Lithuanian-born Jew, Ben-Yehuda immigrated to Israel in 1881. He came with a dream of raising the Hebrew language from the dead. How else could the Jews find their national identity? Their own Land would bring them together, but their own language would keep them together. It was nonnegotiable in his mind. Hebrew must rise from the dead.

So Ben-Yehuda began to develop Modern Hebrew. He used the Scriptures and other ancient sources as his foundation. He scoured libraries for old Hebrew words that fell out of use over the centuries. He taught his wife and insisted only Hebrew be spoken in their home. His newborn son, Ben-Zion, could hear only Hebrew as his first language, which made him the first, native-born speaker of Modern Hebrew!

Ben-Yehuda created Hebrew words for modern needs based on the original root system. As his young son learned the logic of the language, he would also make up words for things around the house. Ben-Yehuda published all of these new words in his weekly Hebrew newspaper. He also created a seventeen-volume dictionary of Modern Hebrew (most of which was published after his death). He developed an intensive method for teaching Hebrew that is still used today. Finally, he created a committee to oversee the ongoing development of the language, which also continues to this day.

Orthodox Jews persecuted Ben-Yehuda for his efforts. They felt Hebrew should not be a secular language, but should be reserved solely for reading Scripture and studying ancient writings. They strongly resisted Ben-Yehuda, ostracizing him and once seeking to kill him. Even Theodor Herzl did not think Ben-Yehuda's dream was possible. Zionists were debating whether German or Yiddish should become their official language. But as more homes and schools caught the dream and taught Hebrew to their children, the modern language that started with a tiny spark spread like fire into the hearts of Jews immigrating to the Land.

In 1921, four years after conquering Jerusalem, the British government recognized Hebrew as one of the three official languages of "Palestine" (along with Arabic and English). Hebrew had been raised from the dead after 1,800 years. Never before had a dead, ancient language been revived to become a modern language. I have no doubt God Himself was behind this striking achievement. A language had been born in a moment, becoming the "sinews" that would hold a nation's "bones" together in their Land.

FROM BARREN TO BEAUTIFUL

"The wilderness and the dry land will be glad; the desert will rejoice and blossom like a wildflower. It will blossom abundantly and will also rejoice with joy and singing" (Isa 35:1-2). Israel's history shouts, "God is a God who gives life to the dead." But so does the very earth where God replanted His people.

When Abram first entered the Land God promised Him, he was met by desert and famine (Gen 12:9-10). So he fled to Egypt with his nephew Lot for the survival of their families and livestock. As they reemerged into Canaan, they realized they had to separate. The land could not sustain both large companies with all their possessions. In a remarkable gesture of generosity and dependence on God, Abram allowed Lot to choose the direction he wanted to settle. So,

> Lot looked around and saw that the whole plain of the Jordan toward Zoar was well watered, like the garden of the Lord, like the land of Egypt. (This was before the Lord destroyed Sodom and Gomorrah.) So Lot chose for himself the whole plain of the Jordan and set out toward the east (Gen 13:10-11, NIV).

Choosing by eyesight and appeal, Lot went where the land boasted irrigation and fertile soil. The lush, emerald vista, rich in natural resources, drew Lot's attention and became the obvious choice. But the obvious choice is not always the best choice. Because Lot chose based only on what he saw, he actually put himself and his family in a dangerous position. The land's abundance and beauty distracted him from the evil that slithered beneath its surface. It would not be long before burning sulfur would wipe out the entire plain that once gushed with life.

Abram, on the other hand, received a Land in stark contrast to Lot's choice. Yet the Land that looked more barren to the natural eye was the Land chosen by God. Abram's portion happened to be the Lord's promise, the place where He would plant His people. The Land of Israel would break forth with rivers in the desert, flow with milk and honey, and burst with natural abundance. The original twelve spies saw this abundance, and the Joshua generation entered into it. What God did for His people in that day, He did again for the reborn nation of the twentieth century.

By the time the British conquered Jerusalem, the Ottomans had been neglecting this Middle Eastern portion of their empire for years. Absentee land-lords and harsh taxes made profitable farming almost impossible. The Holy Land had declined into a vast wasteland. As a piece of physical property, in terms of its natural resources and productivity, Israel was dead.

Mark Twain, in his famous book, *Innocents Abroad*, penned this vivid description of the Holy Land as he traversed its landscape in 1867:

"Of all the lands there are for dismal scenery, I think Palestine must be the prince. The hills are barren, they are dull of color, they are unpicturesque in shape. The valleys are unsightly deserts fringed with a feeble vegetation that has an expression about it of being sorrowful and despondent… There was hardly a tree or a shrub anywhere. Even the olive and the cactus, those fast friends of a worthless soil, had almost deserted the country. A desolation is here that not even imagination can grace with the pomp of life and action."[4]

A few years later, Charles Warren, who spent much time laboring as an archeologist in Jerusalem wrote,

"The Land of Israel is bound up in the chains of its curse which hangs over it. The Land has no redeemer, and it is a wasteland with no one to cultivate it or care for it."[5]

Hundreds of years of wars, conquests, occupations, and neglect had taken its toll on Israel. The stripping away of forests and native vegetation had turned much of the "Beautiful Land" into a swamp. Malaria-carrying mosquitoes overtook the coastal plains and Jordan Valley. As new waves of immigrants poured into Israel in the late nineteenth and early twentieth centuries, they found much of their ancient homeland uninhabitable. Thousands were stricken with malaria.

Yet the God who was raising His nation from the dead of exile, persecution, and Holocaust, would also raise its Land from the death of barrenness. He would be glorified through a desert that would blossom like a wildflower.

When Jews began to return en masse at the end of the nineteenth century, they immediately got to work. Their survival depended on the restoration of the Land. They had to transform this barren region riddled with disease back into "a Land flowing with milk and honey." They founded two major centers for agricultural research and development (one of which exists to this day). They drained the swamps and changed the flow of canals to interrupt the breeding of mosquitoes. Within twenty years after Israel's statehood, the nation was malaria free and positively cultivating its Land.

The seedling nation reintroduced trees and plants native to its soil. It developed cutting-edge technology for irrigation and farming. Farmers adopted the findings of the new research, and the desert began to bloom with the abundance of fruit, grain, nuts, and livestock. Earlier settlers had already established key industries throughout the country. So once it had won its independence and recovered from the war, there stood "Israel"—not as a hope, a dream, or a frail entity fighting for its life—but a modern state among the other nations of the world. History had changed. A nation was reborn and it teemed with life.

Today Israel is one of the largest fruit and flower producers in the Middle East. It is also a major contributor to the world's most important areas of technology: medicine, computing, agriculture, security, and energy. The Land that was once a God-forsaken, barren wilderness is now beautiful beyond description and a blessing to the world. But as much as I respect the ingenuity and sheer determination of the Jewish people, I do not see the modern restoration of Israel as a purely natural occurrence. I believe it is the result of divine providence, intervention, and life-giving power. God had raised this nation from the dead.

> THE LAND THAT WAS ONCE A GOD-FORSAKEN, BARREN WILDERNESS IS NOW BEAUTIFUL BEYOND DESCRIPTION AND A BLESSING TO THE WORLD.

CHAPTER 8

THE GOD WHO GIVES LIFE TO THE DEAD: ISRAEL'S FUTURE

Israel's national resurrection is not its ultimate resurrection. The great prophecies have only *partly* been fulfilled. They are *becoming* fulfilled. But they are not *finally* fulfilled. As miraculous and wonderful as Israel's modern statehood is, the best is yet to come. Imagine the day. Secular and religious Jews from inside and outside the Land of Israel will become Messianic, born-again, Spirit-filled followers of Yeshua. After millennia of rejecting their own gospel, Jews from all over the world will weep in repentance and rejoice in salvation! What a day that will be!

Scripture assures us this day is coming. God is the God who raises the dead. And as we have seen, God has been raising His people from the dead from the very beginning. There's no escape from this glorious, history-ending conclusion. We are on a crash course toward

Israel's ultimate resurrection: spiritual and physical life from the dead as a nation regathered in its own Land. One of the Bible's most compelling prophecies of this grand finale is Ezekiel's vision of the dry bones. So I will dedicate this chapter to that vision. Below I quote it in full, section by section, adding observations I believe are crucial for us to see. I encourage you to read Ezekiel's words carefully. Let their magnitude sink into your heart and inspire your prayers for Israel (Ezek 37:1-14):

> The hand of the Lord was upon me, and He brought me out by the Spirit of the Lord and set me down in the middle of the valley; and it was full of bones. He caused me to pass among them round about, and behold, there were very many on the surface of the valley; and lo, they were very dry. He said to me, "Son of man, can these bones live?" And I answered, "O Lord God, You know." Again He said to me, "Prophesy over these bones and say to them, 'O dry bones, hear the word of the Lord.' Thus says the Lord God to these bones, 'Behold, I will cause breath to enter you that you may come to life. I will put sinews on you, make flesh grow back on you, cover you with skin

and put breath in you that you may come alive;
and you will know that I am the Lord.' "

Did you notice that God did not ask for Ezekiel's permission to take him on this little ride? He just snatched him up and plunked him down in the valley. I doubt Ezekiel had signed up for an excursion through Dead Bones Valley. But that didn't matter. God is the one who oversees His plan for Israel and the world, not Ezekiel or anyone else. Just as God had an appointed time for Sarah to give birth to Isaac, so does He have an appointed time for Israel's resurrection. That is why *He* took the initiative with Ezekiel, and placed him where he could set in motion Israel's rise from the dead.

GOD WILL SPARK THE CHAIN REACTION THAT WILL LEAD TO HIS PEOPLE'S FINAL SALVATION.

God works all things after the counsel of His will. He does not control people's decisions, but He does intervene in history for the redemption of His people—and for the whole world. He will spark the chain reaction that will lead to His people's final salvation. He will not ask permission from the United Nations, the Antichrist, Israel's enemies, or even His own prophets. He will just do it. And I believe He has already started that process.

There's something else we should notice. It was not enough for God to give Ezekiel a little glimpse of Israel's situation. Ezekiel needed a full tour. He needed to see how hopeless—how dead—his people were. From one end of the broad valley floor to the other, over

GOD POSES THE SAME QUESTION TO US THAT HE POSED TO EZEKIEL. CAN THESE BONES LIVE?

every swell and behind every bush, God took Ezekiel on a meticulous inspection of millions of dead, dry bones. Why? The Lord wanted to immerse His prophet into the impossibility of Israel's recovery. The prophet had to know for certain: this simply cannot happen unless God intervenes with almighty, dead-raising power.

God poses the same question to us that He posed to Ezekiel. Can these bones live? But like Ezekiel, we must think before we give the automatic answer, "Of course they can!" We should pause and embrace the reality of Israel's situation so our response can come from a deeper place of faith. Knee-jerk replies will not do. We must be "prophetic," that is, we must allow the Lord to immerse us in His heart and perspective. After all, Ezekiel was not a novice. As a priest, he had been educated in the Torah. As a prophet, he had been submerged in the Holy Spirit's power. He knew the God of Israel well and would have been able to give the correct doctrinal answer. But God was not giving His prophet a Theology 101 quiz. "Ezekiel, can I raise the dead?" // "Yes, Lord, You can raise the dead! // "Correct answer, Ezekiel!"

Ezekiel was not sitting in a Bible school classroom or a comfortable church. He stood in a massive, derelict graveyard. Decayed, unburied bodies lay everywhere. Creatures had picked the corpses clean and time had decomposed them down to skeletons. The bare bones had not been concealed in tombs; they lay scattered all over the ground. The prophet was overwhelmed by the horror and hopelessness. The vision enabled him to see the tragic results of his people's sins and the Lord's anger.

Judgment had come, Judah was devastated, and exiles lived in foreign lands. Zion's children no longer sang in the streets of Jerusalem. They wept in their tombs of dispersion. So a trite, easy answer did not fit here. The prophet had to answer the Lord's question while staring at the bones of a long-dead nation. Only from this vantage point—this immersion into dark calamity and desperation—could the prophet be forced into dependence on the God who raises the dead. Who *must* raise the dead.

We need a similar immersion into Israel's condition. I do not mean that we must see a vision as dramatic as Ezekiel's.

WE CANNOT RAISE THE DEAD THROUGH A POWERLESS CHRISTIANITY.

But we do have Ezekiel's words, and we have access to God's heart by the Spirit. So before we jump into perfunctory prayers, we should become more sober about Israel's situation (1 Pet 4:7). One reason I take people on tours of Israel is so they can see the humanity of the Jewish people. I want people to understand that the "Jews" are not merely a topic of theology. They are human beings, most of whom are spiritually dead and need their Messiah. They still need the Spirit of life to enter them.

Yet these are the very people who must welcome Jesus back to earth. So it's important we catch some sight of the gravity of their situation, but also the wonder of their potential. God wants a people like Ezekiel who will embrace some of His burden. Under the weight of that burden, we will then be compelled into a deeper faith. May God give us a little more of Ezekiel's revelation! We need that push into deeper dependence on God to pray and prophesy Israel out of its grave. The impossible must become reality. The need is greater than we realize. But so is God.

Raising the dead already takes great faith. But this was no ordinary dead raising. What God was asking Ezekiel to do would take even greater faith. Think about the question. "Can these *bones* live?" Ezekiel was not looking at humans that died a few days ago. He was looking only at bones that weren't even skeletons anymore. The "dead" bodies were long gone, degraded all the way down to unrecognizable forms: bones—disassembled and scattered bones. God's word in Ezekiel's mouth would have to be powerful enough to work backwards from a place farther out of reach than death.

First the prophetic word had to assemble the bones. Then the word would have to create dead bodies. *Then* it would have to raise them from the dead! No wonder Ezekiel put the burden back on the Lord. We should heed his example. Like I said, this is no ordinary resurrection. It is the one great resurrection that will spark all others. It will require an immense unleashing of God's creative power.

No human ingenuity or hype will affect the salvation of the Jewish people (or any people, for that matter). We cannot raise the dead through a powerless Christianity. In our image-based society, we have gotten good at producing successful religion without necessarily having the corresponding spiritual life. But we just can't fake resurrection. And we sure can't fake Israel's resurrection. Clever sermons and smoke machines will not work. Jewish unbelief is too deep and their distance from Messiah too great. Only God can raise this nation from the dead. Ezekiel probably knew this before. But now that he's taken the death tour, he really knows it. This is impossible. But that's just when God gives him his assignment. "Prophesy over these bones..."

> *So I prophesied as I was commanded; and as I prophesied, there was a noise, and behold, a rattling; and the bones came together, bone to its bone. And I looked, and behold, sinews were on them, and flesh grew and skin covered them; but there was no breath in them. Then He said to me, "Prophesy to the breath, prophesy, son of man, and say to the breath, 'Thus says the Lord God, "Come from the four winds, O breath, and breathe on these slain, that they come to life."'" So I prophesied as He commanded me, and the breath came into them, and they came to life and stood on their feet, an exceedingly great army.*

What an absolutely phenomenal truth. Not only does this vision show how God "recreates" His chosen people out of raw human materials. And not only does it show how He then breathes on them to raise them from the dead. But it also shows how He uses a human vessel to do it. God is the only one who can raise the dead. His Spirit is the only power that will revive the Jewish people. But God wants to do humanly impossible things *through humans.* When God uses us to do what only God can do, then He is God (2 Cor 4:7). On the day of Israel's salvation,

> ON THE DAY OF ISRAEL'S SALVATION, GOD'S NAME WILL BE HALLOWED LIKE NEVER BEFORE.

God's name will be hallowed like never before. And He will use people like you and me to give Him glory.

Paul tells us that God uses the Gentiles to bring Israel to salvation. Part of their role is to make unbelieving Jews jealous for their own Messiah (Rom 11:11). But God also uses Messianic Jews to bring Israel to salvation. Ezekiel was a Jewish prophet used by God to prophesy to Jewish bones—and then to the Spirit—to trigger a last days' revival of Israel. God is using both believing Gentiles, as well as a holy remnant of Messianic Jews, to revive His people. But either way, it can only happen by the power of the Holy Spirit. Ezekiel was not arguing with the bones. Nor was he pleading with them. *He was prophesying to them in the power of the Holy Spirit.* And that is when they responded. The prophetic word sparked a process that was complete in Israel's salvation.

Look closely at the order of events in this part of the vision. When Ezekiel first prophesied, there was a rattling noise. Bones all around this valley started to vibrate in response to the prophet's voice. There is something deep inside the marrow of this mostly exiled and unbelieving people that will one day recognize the voice of their God when a prophetic people speak by the Spirit. When the Jewish people began to return again from exile in the late 1800s, and then became a state in 1948, most had no idea that they were starting a process that would lead to their ultimate salvation. But their bones knew.

After the bones came together, Ezekiel kept watching. The power of his prophecy had not yet subsided. Once the skeletons formed, then sinews, flesh, and skin came upon them out of the blue. Human bodies were now assembled and clothed—all from one prophecy! But then things came to a halt. Fully formed human beings lay motionless across the valley floor, and Ezekiel made a crucial observation. *"There was no breath in them."*

The first prophecy assembled dry bones and turned them into human bodies. But they had no "breath." I believe this represents the Jews' return from exile—including the modern state of Israel. That return was noisy. "Bones" rattled throughout the nations and snapped together in the Land of Israel, and the whole world heard it. The frames and raw materials of a reborn nation popped into place. *But it still had no spiritual life.* The "breath" of the Messiah had not yet come into them. The first prophetic word had composed the political and natural substructure of God's people. And that was a miracle. It was a partial resurrection. But it was not a *total* resurrection.

THE REVIVAL OF ISRAEL AS A STATE, WITH ITS OWN LANGUAGE AND RICH LAND, HAS BEEN CALLED BACK INTO BEING.

Israel's life-from-the-dead was not yet complete. It was the beginning of a chain reaction that is still in process. We are now between Ezekiel's two prophetic words. The revival of Israel as a state, with its own language and rich Land, has been called back into being. We cannot minimize this aspect of Ezekiel's vision. Israel was an exiled and persecuted people group scattered among the nations. Then they became the target of the worse genocidal attempt in human history—the Holocaust. But somehow they came back to their homeland, reestablished their nation, gathered an army, and fought successfully for their independence. *Only God could do that.*

However, the revival of Israel as a Spirit-filled, Messianic people regathered into its Land from all nations has not yet been called into being. We still await the second phase of Ezekiel's prophetic picture. That is why God told Ezekiel to prophesy again. But this time he prophesied directly to the *ruach,* which is the Hebrew word for "breath," "wind," or "Spirit." God's ultimate expression of life—His *ruach*—then came from the four winds and entered the dead members of Israel's house. They came to life and stood to their feet—an exceedingly great army. This pictures the coming spiritual awakening of the Jewish people. It comes after the natural and political renewal the world has already seen.

> *Then He said to me, "Son of man, these bones are the whole house of Israel; behold, they say, 'Our bones are dried up and our hope has perished. We are completely cut off.' Therefore prophesy and say to them, 'Thus says the Lord God, "Behold, I will open your graves and cause you to come up out of your graves, My people; and I will bring you into the Land of Israel. Then you will know that I am the Lord, when I have opened your graves and caused you to come up out of your graves, My people. I will put My Spirit within you and you will come to life, and I will place you on your own*

Land. Then you will know that I, the Lord, have spoken and done it," declares the Lord.'"

Now the Lord lays it all out for us. He directly interprets the vision He gave Ezekiel. He explains what it means for Israel's future, and that explanation is absolutely breathtaking. God will bring Israel back from a deep, impossible grave. It's a grave that goes deeper than exile. It goes deeper than persecution among the nations. It goes into the depths of a spiritual death caused by a long history of rebellion, persecution, and rejection of their

> DEATH WILL NOT HAVE THE FINAL WORD. GOD WILL. ISRAEL WILL RISE AGAIN.

Messiah. From the belly of these depths, Israel admits its hope has been destroyed and it has been forsaken. There's no one to help.

But the God who has been raising the dead since the beginning will call these dead back to life—even from the farthest reaches of Sheol. The God who made a covenant with Abraham, Isaac, and Jacob will honor His covenant. The darker death's shadow, the more glory God will receive when He calls this final Lazarus out of the tomb. Death will not have the final word. God will. Israel will rise again. This is the promise on which we base our hope, our prayers, and our efforts of ministry. We do not look at what is seen. We look to God's yet unseen promise of Israel's life from the dead.

I know that people interpret this passage in different ways. I do not claim to know the exact timeline of all of these events. But I do believe that the process of Israel's life from the dead has already begun. The second part of Ezekiel's vision—the spiritual resurrection—was partially fulfilled when an upper room of 120 Jews received the Holy Spirit at Pentecost. Divine breath came into them and they lived. They stood to their feet as a small beginning of Ezekiel's great army. Yet their impact was still enormous. Their witness brought that same breath to thousands more Jews in Jerusalem that very day. Jewish people in their Land believed in their Messiah and received the breath of new life. Thousands more were added in the days and years ahead before Jerusalem's fall in 70 AD. The breath has started to come.

Now again after a centuries-long night of exile, Jews have returned to their Land as a reconstituted army without breath. But the Spirit is slowly filling their lungs. About 20,000 Messianic Jews live in the Land of Israel (most of whom immigrated). Among these, fewer than 5,000 are native-born Israelis. One church-planting missionary in Israel told me that number could be as few as 1,500. Either way, that is not an exceedingly great army. But it is a start. The

Spirit of life has come into Jews who live in Israel. The first phase of Ezekiel's vision has been fulfilled again in our era, and the second phase continues through the Gospel. The stage is set for the ultimate fulfillment.

ALL OF ISRAEL WILL BE ALIVE FROM THE DEAD IN THEIR OWN LAND. AND THAT EVENT WILL LAUNCH THE FINAL VICTORY OVER DEATH.

That is why the Lord promises the ultimate fulfillment in the last verse. He declares that He will put His Spirit within His people, they will come to life, and God will place them on their own Land. But hasn't that already happened? Yes, Jews have returned to their Land more than once. Yet most still live outside the Land of Israel. The Lord is telling Ezekiel, as He has also told other prophets, that a day is coming when all Jews outside the Land of Israel will turn to Him, receive the Spirit, and return to their Land (Jer 29:14; Ezek 37:15-28). I do not know exactly what that will look like, but I know it will happen. *All* of Israel will be alive from the dead in their own Land. And that event will launch the final victory over death.

This is why we pray for Israel's salvation. God will fulfill His covenant with His people—not only because He loves them, but also because He loves all nations and people just as much. So to fulfill His plan for them—to raise all believers from the dead, judge the nations, and renew heaven and earth—*He must first bring about Israel's salvation.*

Jesus told the people of Jerusalem who rejected Him, "Look! Your house is left to you deserted. For I tell you: you surely will not see me from now on *until* you say, 'Blessed is He who comes in the name of the Lord' " (Matt 23:38-39). On the one hand, this meant judgment. The Jews would be exiled again and their temple destroyed. But on the other hand, this meant hope—with a caveat. Jerusalem will not see its Messiah again *until* its people welcome Him back. But they *will* see Him! Their repentance will bring Him back.

This is why Peter told Jews in the temple to "repent and return, so that your sins may be wiped away, in order that times of refreshing may come from the presence of the Lord; *and that He may send Jesus*, the Christ appointed for you, whom heaven must receive until the period of restoration of all things about which God spoke by the mouth of His holy prophets from ancient time" (Acts 3:19-21).

Dr. Michael Brown writes about this holy sequence: "If *every* eye will see Him when He returns, and if Jerusalem *will not see Him* until she welcomes Him back, then *no eye* will see Him until Jerusalem receives Him!"[1] Jesus will return to earth only after His own people welcome Him. Paul says, "For if [Israel's] rejection brought reconciliation to the world, what will their acceptance be *but life from the dead?"* (Rom 11:15). That's the divine order, and that's our theme: God is the God who raises the dead. He will raise His people, Israel, from their spiritual death. Their national repentance will bring Jesus back to earth, which will precipitate

JESUS WILL RETURN TO EARTH ONLY AFTER HIS OWN PEOPLE WELCOME HIM.

the restoration of all things—a restoration that includes the final resurrection and final judgment. The righteous will inherit eternal life and the earth will be totally renewed. That is quite a chain of events. And it all depends on the salvation of Israel. Their spiritual resurrection initiates the Day of the Lord.

What can we say to these things? Without the salvation of Israel, God's eternal purpose does not come to fruition. The entire Body, the One New Man consisting of both Jews and Gentiles, must unite in our corporate likeness of Messiah. This will bring about the "fullness of the Gentiles," draw Israel to the Messiah, and revive Israel through the Spirit. So let's invest in Israel's salvation. This is no trivial doctrinal matter. This is life or death. Actually, this is life *out of* death. Let us, therefore, apply ourselves to God's promise. Even though He is the one to initiate its fulfillment, we, like Ezekiel, must partner with Him when He does. The next chapter gives us some practical ways to do just that.

CHAPTER 9

HOW THEN SHALL
WE LIVE?

A ROOM WITH A VIEW

It seems providential that I write this final chapter from a hotel room overlooking the city of Jerusalem. As I peer out my tenth floor window at the "city of the great King" (Psa 48:2), I am struck by its contrasting views. All looks beautiful and peaceful from the height of my room. The various shades of Jerusalem stone color the cityscape. Cars drive and people walk through streets and alleys going about their business. It's an extraordinary sight. The compact city mingles ancient structures, modern amenities, and all sorts of people to create a genuine charm and outward harmony. There is no sign to the natural eye of the restlessness that abides within.

But once I descend to the ground level, my perspective changes. Jerusalem's contradictions are stark,

155

perhaps foreboding. The Old City squeezes into less than one square mile. Yet it is divided into four quarters: the Christian Quarter, Jewish Quarter, Muslim Quarter, and Armenian Quarter. This fact alone indicates the tension of a city divided culturally, politically, and religiously. Ultraorthodox Jewish men, clad in black suits and hats, cross the street beside Muslim women wearing hijabs. Devout Jewish people pray at the Western Wall while the Muslim call to prayer blasts through loudspeakers overhead.

BUT WE DO NOT BLESS ISRAEL FROM A NATURAL POINT OF VIEW. WE BLESS ISRAEL FROM A SCRIPTURAL POINT OF VIEW.

Tension lies just below the surface of the city's superficial "peace." Hardly any Jews in Jerusalem know their Messiah. Muslims deny that God can even have a Son, and many of the city's "Christians" practice a very traditional and even superstitious religion. Meanwhile these spiritual contrasts coincide with the political friction that permeates the atmosphere. Jerusalem is scarcely a praise in the earth. Neither this city, nor this nation, has yet arrived at its destiny.

Such a natural perspective will never motivate us to bless Israel. If we look at Jerusalem from the ground level alone, without also looking from God's higher perspective, we have no reason to go out of our way to bless this nation. But we do not bless Israel from a natural point of view. We bless Israel from a scriptural point of view.

THE CHURCH'S CALL
TO BLESS ISRAEL

From Scripture's higher view, Jerusalem's broken condition becomes the very reason we *should* bless Israel. The Bible tells us that without Israel's spiritual resurrection, God's plan will not be accomplished; and Jesus will not return. That alone should compel the global Church to bless Israel. Paul made this clear to his Gentile churches. He urged them to pray for Israel's salvation, to proclaim the truth about Israel, to provide for Israel, and to provoke Israel to jealousy.

Paul taught these things, not merely as a Jew, but as an apostle. He carried a revelation of God's purposes and how they applied to the Church's life. He knew that an attitude of blessing toward Israel was part of the Church's foundation and mission. His mostly Gentile churches could not afford to take a posture of ignorance or anti-Semitism toward Israel. Rather, they had to heed the call to bless Israel—for their own sake, for Israel's sake, and for the world's sake.

Let us return to this apostolic perspective. Even while many Jews act like enemies of the Gospel, they are still beloved. They are still recipients of God's covenant with the fathers (Rom 11:28). Their promises will still come to pass when they turn to Messiah. Therefore, they remain our lost, elder brother. We should mourn our brother's estrangement, not curse it. We should long for his restoration, not ignore it. Like the father of the prodigal son, we should await our brother's return with a posture of blessing.

After all, God promises to bless those who bless Israel. And His promises are as firm as Mount Zion. He told a man past his prime with a barren wife, "I will make you a great nation" (Gen 12:2), and that's exactly what He did. Then He said, "I will bless those who bless you..." (Gen 12:3); and He has been fulfilling that promise for thousands of years. If He accomplished the first impossible promise, He will continue to fulfill the second. When God says, "I will," He means, "I will." God will bless us when we bless Israel. Here, then, are four practical ways we can bless Israel.

PRAY

Brethren, my heart's desire and my prayer to God for [Israel] is for their salvation (Rom 10:1).

Simply put, we can bless Israel when we pray for their salvation. Sometimes the Church doesn't know how to pray for Israel. So offers us a simple prayer. Just pray for their salvation! As Jesus taught, God does not hear us for our many words anyway. But He does hear us when our hearts are invested.

> SIMPLY PUT, WE CAN BLESS ISRAEL WHEN WE PRAY FOR THEIR SALVATION.

That is why Paul's wording is important. Before he mentions his prayer for Israel's salvation, he first mentions his heart's desire. Paul does not pray out of rote obligation. He prays out of deep yearning. He longs for Israel to be saved. Paul shares God's intense burden for His "firstborn son," Israel, to come home (Exod 4:22). That is why his prayer for Israel touches God's heart.

Recently a friend called to tell me he was standing with me in prayer. He said he prayed daily for every member of our family by name. He then asked about each one of my children. He wanted to focus on their particular needs to pray more effectively. My heart was immediately endeared to this brother. He did not call to get something from me. He called to serve my family—particularly my children. With clear compassion and burden, my friend wanted to pray that my sons and daughters would flourish in every way. Few things could encourage my father's heart more. Someone out there cares so much for my kids that he pray sacrificially for them by name. I was deeply moved.

If that is how I, an earthly father, feel about someone praying for my children, how much more does our heavenly Father delight in our prayers for Israel, His firstborn son? What joy it must bring God's heart to know the Church shares His burden to bring His eldest son home. And what power such prayers carry! When the Church cares for God's firstborn the way He does—and then prays out of that concern—it can actually hasten the Lord's return.

> IF YOU DON'T FEEL LIKE YOU SHARE GOD'S HEART FOR ISRAEL, ASK HIM FOR HIS BURDEN.

If you don't feel like you share God's heart for Israel, ask Him for His burden. He would love to share it with you! Pursue His heart by praying through passages from Scripture. But as you do, don't just think of the words. Think also that the One to whom you direct those words loves Israel and longs for their salvation. That will temper the way you pray. You will be surprised at how soft your heart will get for His people. Pray for Israel's salvation (Rom 10:1). Pray for Jerusalem's peace (Psa 122:6; Isa 62:6-7). Pray for believers in the Land (Matt 9:36-10:23). Pray for the last days' outpouring of the Spirit (Zech 12:10).

I encourage you to make time every day to pray over these passages. And I encourage churches to include intercession for Israel in their prayer meetings. Even better, consider dedicating one night per week or month just to pray for Israel's salvation. These sacrifices will deeply touch God's heart. They will also be a blessing to Israel. And God will bless you as a result.

PROCLAIM

> *[Paul and Silas] came to Thessalonica, where there was a synagogue of the Jews. And as was his custom, Paul went in to them and on three Sabbath days he discussed with them from the Scriptures, explaining and demonstrating that it was necessary for the Messiah to suffer and to rise from the dead, and saying, "This Jesus whom I am proclaiming to you is the Messiah" (Acts 17:1-3, CSB).*

> *I am not ashamed of the Gospel, for it is the power of God for salvation to everyone who believes, to the Jew first and also to the Greek (Rom 1:16).*

Proclamation blesses Israel in two ways. First, and most importantly, we must proclaim the gospel to Jewish people. The Church must make that our priority again. It's ironic that, in the first century, some Jews struggled to believe that Gentiles could come into their Messianic faith. Now some Gentiles struggle to believe Jews can come into their Christian faith. What a reversal! Paul's words should get us back in tune with God's priorities. The Jews are not our afterthought; they are God's forethought. The Gospel is first for them.

THE JEWS ARE NOT OUR AFTERTHOUGHT; THEY ARE GOD'S FORETHOUGHT.

But that does not mean Jews are more important than Gentiles. There are no first and second classes in the Church. Paul is honoring God's covenant with the Jews, as well as His plan for them. They have priority, not for themselves, but *to serve the nations*. So the order is important both for Jews and Gentiles. Yet Paul must also resist the Church's tendency to ignore the Jews—or even reject them. That is why he says "to the Jew first." We should heed Paul's words. Why is so much of the Church content to ignore Jews in their outreach efforts? According to Scripture, they should be first in our efforts.

Some cities have Jewish neighborhoods. Local churches should pray about Gospel outreaches there (Matt 10). Otherwise we can always pray for divine appointments. The Lord has given me wonderful, impromptu opportunities to share Jesus with Jewish people. From a cab driver in Israel to a well-known businessman in America, those divine encounters were precious times to sow Gospel seeds into the chosen people.

Second, we must proclaim the truth about Israel to the Church. Historic anti-Semitism and replacement theology have turned the minds of many Christians away from God's heart for Israel. But proclaiming the scriptural truth can reverse that. I encourage pastors to teach an annual series about Israel's unique role in God's plan. Church members can do small-group book studies that focus on Israel.[1] The more we raise awareness in the Church about God's covenant with Israel, the better equipped the Church will be to fulfill God's plan.

PROVIDE

For Macedonia and Achaia have been pleased to make a contribution for the poor among the saints in Jerusalem... For if the Gentiles have shared in [Israel's] spiritual blessings, they owe it to [Israel] to share with them their material blessings (Rom. 15:26-27).

We bless Israel by helping to support needy believers in the Land. Paul viewed this as a crucial part of his mission. He had been planting churches that consisted of some Jews but mostly Gentiles. He discovered that Jewish and Gentile believers did not always get along very well in these churches. They had come from radically different backgrounds that made it challenging to blend into a new spiritual family.

In fact, this is one major reason Paul wrote his letter to the Romans. He wanted Jewish believers to understand that God accepts Gentiles by faith, not by works of the Law. Believers from the nations were no longer outsiders. They were brothers and sisters, sharing the same status as Messianic Jews. But Paul also wanted Gentiles to understand that Jews still held a special place in God's heart and plan. Even though most had rejected the Gospel, the mostly Gentile Church had not replaced Israel. Instead, Messianic Israel was now welcoming many Gentiles into their New Covenant. And one day all of Israel will be saved!

In the meantime, a new kind of family had formed. Paul wanted believers from both camps—Jews and Gentiles—to show one another equal love and honor. If Jews and Gentiles could become one family in the

Messiah, then Jesus really was Lord. What a testimony to the rest of the world!

But what does all of this have to do with giving money? Paul knew a powerful way Gentiles could express their solidarity with Messianic Jews was to help them financially in their time of need. Many Jewish believers in Israel were experiencing hardship. So Paul worked to harvest an offering from the Gentile Churches and deliver it to the poor of Jerusalem. He knew it would be a compelling act of unity.

> OUR FINANCIAL PROVISION TO BELIEVERS IN ISRAEL IS MORE THAN A MONETARY ISSUE. IT'S A DEEPLY SPIRITUAL ISSUE.

We among the nations should do the same thing today. Our financial provision to believers in Israel is more than a monetary issue. It's a deeply spiritual issue. It is a sacrificial act of worship to God because it honors His desire for "one new man" (Eph 2:15). What better way to show our union with God and His people than to support our needy brothers and sisters in Israel?

I am grieved when funds raised for Israel never actually find their way into the hands of believers. A major Christian magazine recently devoted an entire article to this tragic failure. It's time that trend turns around and we start lining up with the biblical mandate of Romans 15:27. It encourages my heart to know there are churches in the West that receive regular offerings for the saints in Israel, funneling them through organizations that give directly to believers in the Land.

Together For Israel is an organization dedicated to channeling funds to Jewish and Arab believers in the Land who have serious needs, who labor in the Gospel, or both. We have no greater joy than to see the Lord provide for these "saints in Jerusalem" (and all over the Land of Israel) through our work. We bless Israel indeed when we bless them in need.

PROVOKE

Salvation has come to the Gentiles, to make them jealous... I am speaking to you who are Gentiles. Inasmuch then as I am an apostle of Gentiles, I magnify my ministry, if somehow I might move to jealousy my fellow countrymen and save some of them (Rom 11:11, 13-14).

A good friend of mine told me how he came to believe in Messiah. He was a teenage Jew with no interest in religion. But his mother cajoled him to attend a Pentecostal Church with her. (She had gotten saved some months before.) Everything about it made him uncomfortable. People worshipped loudly. They raised their hands to sing and pray. One lady's face flowed with tears as she cried out, "Jesus!" over and over. After a Bible-based message from the pastor, people came to the front of the room to pray out loud again. Nothing was private or subdued. My friend hated it. He thought it was a cult.

But a small hook caught his heart. He had to admit there was something different about these folks. They were weird, yes. But they were not just weird. Something else made them different. They seeped with sincerity. Nothing about them was fake. All of it was genuine: faith, forgiveness, and family. My friend became intrigued. So that first visit turned into a couple more over the next month or so. The hook got deeper.

As he got to know them better, my friend discovered these quirky hand raisers really cared for one another. They exuded eternal purpose and peace; they had more hope than fear. They admitted their imperfections but were also very good people. Their lives were pure; they loved everyone; they refused to judge outsiders. My friend got addicted to their fellowship.

After some time, it dawned on him that these people were in fact "saved" in some sense. He could tell they were alive in a way other people were not. They possessed real life—a life the world could not offer, and a life he did not share. This made him *jealous.* He wanted what they had. He coveted the divine life they possessed. So my Jewish friend gave his heart to the Jesus those people worshipped. And he has been enjoying that same life ever since.

THE CHURCH SHOULD MAKE JEWISH PEOPLE ENVY WHAT THEY HAVE!

Did you know that God has called Gentile believers to provoke Israel to that same jealousy? The Church should make Jewish people envy what they have! Unfortunately, the exact opposite has happened throughout the centuries. Rather than provoking Israel to a godly jealousy, Israel has often been provoked to anger. People who called themselves Christians have abused the Jewish people rather than loved them. As a result, Jews have associated "Christianity" with an aberrant Gentile religion that inspired their persecution—and even their destruction. The halls of Church history are littered with the dust of anti-Semitism.

It is time to reverse that tragic history. It is time for the Church to make Israel *jealous* by the life we possess through their Messiah. How do we do that? Paul answers that question. He says he "magnifies" his ministry. More literally he "glorifies" his ministry. That's the positive way of saying what he told the

Romans earlier—that he was "not ashamed of the Gospel." Paul did not hide the Gospel out of shame; he glorified it with honor. He did not pretend to be a typical religious Jew while hiding his belief in Yeshua. There was nothing private about his faith. No matter how much his kinsmen devalued his proclamation, he knew he could never make them envious if they intimidated him into silence. He magnified his ministry.

Likewise, we cannot be timid about our faith in the Jewish Messiah. We cannot hide our glorious life in His Spirit. This is the exact spiritual life God intended for the Jews. How can we hide it from them? We must "glorify" it. If we do not embody the Messiah's Gospel publicly, we cannot make Jews jealous.

Paul based his comments about jealousy on Moses' words to obstinate Israel: "I will provoke you to jealousy by those who are not a nation" (Rom 10:19; cf. Deut 32:21). Paul read that verse and responded, "I will do that! I will magnify my ministry to the nations to make my people jealous!" But this jealousy would be a good thing. It would lead to the salvation of "some of them" (Rom 11:14). So must our Gospel faith. We cannot make Israel jealous from a church building. We must magnify our ministry!

That is why I offer practical tools to bless Israel: *pray, proclaim,* and *provide.* Because by doing these things, I hope we can also *provoke* some Jews to jealousy.

But that provocation will only come through a supernatural life worthy of jealousy! Thus Paul exhorts the Romans to offer their bodies as living sacrifices, wholly surrendered to God (Rom 12:1-3; see also Rom 6-8). When we live a life fully immersed in the Spirit—in love, holiness, faith, and power—we will give Israel something to envy.

We cannot make Jews jealous through powerless, religious, Sunday-morning Christianity. Neither will we provoke them if we continue historic anti-Semitism or replacement theologies. No, we are called to love them sincerely and sacrificially. We must possess the *life* of the Spirit that drew my Jewish friend to his Messiah. We must then unveil the power of that life the way Ezekiel prophesied to the dry bones. There is no other way to make Israel jealous. They must look at us and see the covenant blessings they lack. Only then will they become jealous for what we have. Only then will they see their Messiah in us.

ABOUT THE AUTHORS

Scott Volk is the founder and director of Together for Israel (TFI), a nonprofit ministry that exists to support believers laboring in the land of Israel (Rom 15:25-27). As a Messianic Jew who came to faith in 1975, Scott graduated from North Central University in Minneapolis in 1988 and served in various pastoral capacities in Arizona, Florida, and North Carolina before he devoted himself to overseeing TFI full time in 2012.

Scott and his wife Beth have been married for thirty-one years. They have five children and reside in Charlotte, North Carolina.

Bob Gladstone and his wife, Jeana, lead a growing group of house churches in Charlotte, NC called the King's People. Bob has taught at the Brownsville Revival School of Ministry and Fire School of Ministry. He holds a PhD in New Testament from Logos University, and speaks at churches, conferences, and Bible schools about God's Kingdom. Bob and Jeana have been married for thirty-three years. They have five children and one grandson.

VISIT OUR
NEW WEBSITE!

LEARN ABOUT OUR WORK
LISTEN TO PODCASTS
READ OUR BLOGS
DONATE

WWW.TOGETHERFORISRAEL.ORG

The
TOGETHER FOR
ISRAEL
Mobile App

WEEKLY PODCASTS

TEACHING SERIES

READING PLANS

PRAYER POINTS

VIDEOS

AND MORE!

SEARCH 'TOGETHER FOR ISRAEL' IN THE APP STORE

ORIGINS
BIBLE STUDY

4 -WEEK INDIVIDUAL
OR SMALL GROUP STUDY

When we talk about the origins of our faith, it's
vitally important to go back to the very beginning
of time in order to understand who Jesus is and
why the Lord sent Him...

ORDER YOUR COPY ON THE TFI APP
OR WEBSITE TODAY!

WWW.TOGETHERFORISRAEL.ORG

TFI TOURS

ONE TRIP TO ISRAEL WILL TRANSFORM YOU FOR A LIFETIME.

JOIN US AS WE VISIT THE MAJOR BIBLICAL SITES AND LEARN OF THE HISTORICAL SIGNIFICANCE AS WELL AS THE BIBLICAL RELEVANCE OF EACH LOCATION

GO BEHIND-THE-SCENES AND VISIT MANY PLACES THAT A TYPICAL TOUR WILL NOT GO, LIKE AN UNDERPRIVILEGED CHILDREN'S CENTER, ATTENDING A TORAH TEACHING BY AN ORTHODOX RABBI AND MORE!

NOT ONLY DOES TFI HOST ANNUAL TOURS OF THE HOLY LAND, BUT WE ALSO PARTNER WITH CHURCHES AND MINISTRIES AND ORGANIZE AND TAILOR A TOUR SPECIFICALLY FOR THEM.

LEARN MORE AT WWW.TFI.TOURS

TOGETHER FOR
ISRAEL

TO LEARN MORE ABOUT TFI, DONATE OR
INVITE SCOTT TO SPEAK AT YOUR
EVENT, EMAIL US AT:

INFO@TOGETHERFORISRAEL.ORG

SCAN HERE TO MAKE
A DONATION.

ENDNOTES

Chapter 1

[1] *The Jewish New Testament*, translated by David H. Stern (Baltimore: Jewish New Testament Publications, 1989).

Chapter 7

[1] *Against All Odds: Israel Survives (Episode Six)*, directed by American Trademark Pictures, 2006.
[2] Mitchell G. Bard, *Myths and Facts: A Guide to the Arab-Israeli Conflict* (Chevy Chase: AICE, 2017). www.jewishvirtuallibrary.org/jsource/images/mf2017.pdf#page=43
[3] Hela Crown-Tamir, *Israel, History in a Nutshell: Highlighting the Wars and Military History* (Jerusalem: TsurTsina Publications: 2012) 17.
[4] Mark Twain, *The Innocents Abroad* (Hartford: The American Publishing Company: 1895) 606, 555, 520.
[5] Ari Enkin, "The Land Needs the Jews!" *United with Israel*, November 10, 2014, https://unitedwithisrael.org/the-land-needs-the-jews/.

Chapter 8

[1] Michael Brown, *Our Hands Are Stained with Blood: The Tragic Story of the "Church" and the Jewish People* (Shippensburg: Destiny Image, 1990) 167.

Chapter 9

[1] I suggest Dr. Michael Brown's *Our Hands Are Stained with Blood* (Shippensburg: Destiny Image, 1990); Dan Juster's *Jewish Roots: Understanding Your Jewish Faith,* Revised Edition (Shippensburg: Destiny Image, 2013); David Harwood's *For the Sake of the Fathers: A New Testament View of God's Love for the Jewish People* (Createspace, 2018); or Sandra Teplinsky's *Why Still Care about Israel?* (Grand Rapids: Baker, 2013).